Confessions
of a Prairie Pilgrim

Confessions

OF A PRAIRIE PILGRIM

Woodie W. White

ABINGDON PRESS
NASHVILLE

CONFESSIONS OF A PRAIRIE PILGRIM

Copyright © 1988 by Woodie W. White

This book is printed on acid-free paper.

Library of Congress Cataloging-in-Publication Data

WHITE, WOODIE W., 1935-
    Confessions of a prairie pilgrim.
    1. White, Woodie W., 1935- . 2. United Methodist Church (U.S.)—Doctrines. 3. Methodist Church—United States—Doctrines. I. Title.
BX8331.2.W52   1988   287'.6   87-15903

ISBN 0-687-09391-0 (alk. paper)

Scripture quotations in this publication unless otherwise noted are from the Revised Standard Version of the Bible, copyrighted 1946, 1952, © 1971, 1973 by the Division of Christian Education of the National Council of the Churches of Christ in the U.S.A., and are used by permission.

Scripture quotations marked NEB are from The New English Bible. Copyright © the Delegates of the Oxford University Press and the Syndics of the Cambridge University Press 1961, 1970. Reprinted by permission.

MANUFACTURED BY THE PARTHENON PRESS AT
NASHVILLE, TENNESSEE, UNITED STATES OF AMERICA

To

the precious people of the Illinois Area of
The United Methodist Church

*"I was a stranger
and you welcomed me"*

CONTENTS

For everything there is a season, and a time for every matter under heaven:

   a time to be born, and a time to die;
   a time to plant, and a time to pluck
     up what is planted . . .
   a time to weep, and a time to laugh;
   a time to mourn, and a time to dance . . .
   a time to embrace, and a time to
     refrain from embracing;
   a time to seek, and a time to lose . . .
   a time to rend, and a time to sew;
   a time to keep silence, and a time to speak . . .

Ecclesiastes 3:1-7 (RSV)

F O R E W O R D

*H*e was an urban man. He is now a man of the Midwest prairie.

Born and raised in New York City, Woodie W. White, after graduating from Paine College in Georgia, spent his life as a student and cleric in Boston, Detroit, Baltimore, and Washington, D.C.

Then at the age of forty-eight he was elected bishop of The United Methodist Church in 1984 at Duluth, Minnesota, and was assigned to the predominately town and country Illinois Episcopal Area of the denomination.

A mood of excitement rippled through the area after his assignment. Sometimes anxious—how would our first ethnic minority bishop be received?—most times anticipatory, his spirit and strong leadership were well known.

I had met him a couple of times before his arrival in Springfield, notably in Duluth when I covered the episcopal elections for the church and public press in "downstate Illinois." Then I spent an afternoon with him soon after his taking up his new duties.

"Would you like to write a column for the Central Illinois Conference newspaper?" I asked. As editor of the conference edition of *The United Methodist Reporter,* I wanted him to have the opportunity to communicate weekly with church members and clergy. I expected he might write an article every month or two.

"I've never done anything like that, but let me think about it," he said, his countenance bright, his eyes eager. Before I left that day, he had given me his answer: He wanted to try a weekly column. The deadlines might find him in airports, in Stockholm or Nairobi, in a meeting—even the Council of Bishops—but his telephone calls to deliver his article or his mailed handwritten copy always arrived on time.

This book is a result of his written conversations with the "people of God" on the prairie over a two year period. It has been a memorable and rewarding experience for me to work with him in editing the original pieces as well as having been the freelance editor for this volume.

The response to his written conversations has been overwhelming. Letters pour in to Bishop White in Springfield and to me at the conference communications office in Bloomington. Church members and pastors share touching stories that were drawn out by something he wrote. Or they want him to know, "Yes, that's the way it is with me." Or they argue with him over a view he holds, sometimes vehemently violent in their opposition. They teach him about farm life and what is driven down a soybean field at night. They urge him to give up his eastern loyalties and become a Cub or Cardinal baseball fan or University of Illinois football fan. They write a clever spoof on one of his pieces. They use his writings as a basis for church school class discussions, clip them to share with others or to read over and over. Requests come in regularly for reprint rights from this region and from across the country.

His acceptance into the hearts of the people is

shown when he appears, sometimes unexpected, in local churches. "I feel at home, instantly accepted, as if they have known me as a close friend for a long time," he says. "It's unbelievable. It has to be the result of the column."

The key, it seems to me, is that he shares his own vulnerability, his humanness, and his insights of faith with humor in everyday situations. He cajoles and challenges, praises and presses us to strive toward the good, and he shows his journey with us in that striving. He demonstrates his love for flawed human beings—we all have in common the label of sinner, he says—but by naming us the "precious people of God," he calls us beyond ourselves to live life with Christ in its wholeness.

Join this urban and rural prairie pilgrim in the journey.

Bettie Wilson Story
Editor

INTRODUCTION

*L*ife has an inescapable wholeness. The temptation is to fashion it into our image of what life ought to be. The pessimist sees only the dark side of life, the optimist only the bright. However, life is both light and darkness, laughter and tears, sadness and joy.

Some religions or religionists possess a proclivity to rearrange human experience in such a way as to make life one-sided, often a dull and unfriendly existence. Like a china shop with expensive, beautiful china marked "Do Not Touch," life is to be guarded, protected, observed—not lived or experienced.

Such a view of life inevitably moves toward its dichotimization, sometimes called sacred and secular. The righteous people engage in sacred activity, the not so righteous secular, thus robbing life of its wholeness.

Fundamentally, that's what bigotry does: It attempts to remove certain people from the center of life because of their color or gender, belief or class, language or ethnicity, and sets them on the edge of life. Sometimes they are abused, oppressed, or simply ignored. Their life experiences become homogenized and one-dimensional. They lack interaction and diversity and are soon void of wholeness.

Life is rich because of its wholeness, its cycles and variety. Variety is not the "spice of life," but life itself. Some attempt to avoid this essential characteristic of life only to discover the futility of seeking to escape the inescapable. Some pay a heavy cost before learning this reality; others are fortunate, and the toll is minimal.

I don't remember when I learned about the ambiguities of life. I have discovered that if one cannot learn to live in their midst, one could soon be overwhelmed by them. "Good" people do bad things and "bad" people do good things. The wicked do prosper. And like Paul, the good we ought and want to do is the very thing we fail to do, and the wrong we don't want to do is too often the very thing we do. Goodness is no assurance against tragedy.

My faith has taught me about the wholeness of life—how to embrace it, learn from it, give to it. I shudder to think what I would do without it. Without Jesus, who is the center and foundation of my faith, mountains would be insurmountable, valleys too deep, sorrows too great, burdens too heavy.

As I meet life in its wholeness with its joys and pains, life and death, certainty and ambiguity, I am at one with Paul in declaring:

> Who shall separate us from the love of Christ? Shall tribulation, or distress, or persecution, or famine, or nakedness, or peril, or sword? . . . No, in all these things we are more than conquerors through him who loved us. For I am sure that neither death, nor life, nor angels, nor principalities, nor things present, nor things to come, nor powers, nor height, nor depth, nor anything else in all creation, will be able to separate us from the love of God in Christ Jesus our Lord. (Romans 8:35, 37-39)

Come now, walk with me awhile in the wholeness of life, and you may discover that you have been there, too.

Your servant in Christ,
Woodie W. White

Confessions
of a Prairie Pilgrim

THE SPRING OF
PERSONAL DISCIPLINE

I have often found that the sense of the Presence of God may not always be experienced in prayer and in meditation. . . . Then there are other times when one has the sense of being invaded by the Spirit of God even though one is not involved in any of the disciplines.

. . . An important function of the [spiritual] exercises is to build an immunity against the confusion and the distractions of environment. They seem to make a clearing in the woods in which one may be still . . . that the tryst may be kept with the Spirit. They do not guarantee that the Spirit will be encountered but they do prepare the way of response to its movement.

"Take the dimness of my soul away"—this seems to be the central function of spiritual exercises. This is enough! Enough!

—Howard Thurman
Meditations of the Heart

A TIME TO PLANT IN EXPECTANCY

I saw a light in the distance; it came closer and closer. What was a car doing in the soybean field? *That's ridiculous,* I thought, but the light continued to move closer.

"Kim," I called. "There's a car in the soybean field!"

She laughed. "It's a tractor, dummy!" (Imagine calling a bishop "dummy"!)

I did not know that farmers worked in fields at night. What's more, this one was plowing (is that the correct term?) "my" soybean field.

My daily ritual is to go each morning to the kitchen window and look at "my" field. Now this farmer was plowing it up. He was getting ready for a new year.

I have been thinking a great deal about farming and have been making interesting observations about farmers and farming. It never occurred to me how vulnerable farmers are. Although they prepare, cultivate, and eventually harvest their crops, they are dependent on so many factors beyond their control. Too much rain or not enough rain can devastate even the best farmer's efforts. A bitter or unseasonably cold winter, like that experienced several years ago by Florida farmers, can have disastrous effects on crops.

Since coming to Illinois, I have listened with new interest to farm news and price reports each morning. I don't fully understand, but I gather that prices vary daily.

Imagine those of us who are on fixed or agreed upon salaries having to check each day to determine what our salary would be. It's pretty frightening to contemplate. So the farmer moves with uncertainty, hope, and faith into the future.

Farmers must plan carefully. Often they work from sunup to well into night. They give all they can physically, emotionally, and financially. Yet they are vulnerable. They wait, trust, hope, and I'm sure they pray.

As I looked out my kitchen window that night, I became aware that the farmer was readying the soil for a new year. Perhaps I'll see corn next year. If so, I will miss the soybeans out my window.

How will you approach the new year? Look afresh at it now. Don't be so tied to the disappointments and difficulties of last year that they shape your view of the new one. Like the farmer, prepare with a sense of hope and expectancy. See the future as open with marvelous, fresh opportunities for good.

That soybean field of "mine" is now leveled. There's a cleanness about it, each row neatly plowed. It's an opportunity to start again.

I hope the new year will be for you a fresh start, a new beginning, a clean slate. Do all in your power to make it a good year. Plant seeds of love and good will, compassion and understanding, openness and forgiveness, giving and generosity.

As you plant your seeds for the new year and cultivate them with prayer, meditation, reflection, and hard work, remember your vulnerability to that which is outside your power to control. To live is to be vulnerable, but do all in your power to make life a fulfilling and meaningful experience.

After you have done all in your power, you must realize that the rest belongs to another power. Therefore, move into this new year with hope and with faith. Most of all, face it with the assurance that you do not face it alone.

Remember the words of our Lord, ". . . Lo, I am with you always."

PRAYER IS A VITAL REALITY

In my calendar, I have written the name of a district in the Illinois Area on each day and circled it in red. This is my prayer reminder. Each day I pray for one of our districts. I call by name the district superintendent, and I hold before God the pastors, their families, and the people in the local churches. In that way, I enter their lives and their ministries. Tennyson said, "More things are wrought by prayer than the world dreams of."

Howard Thurman and Henri J. M. Nouwen have been my two most important teachers in the area of prayer and meditation. They are two constant companions. They know how to talk to God.

During one of my district visits and dialogues, a pastor asked me, "How do you blow off steam?"

Without hesitating, I said, "I worry God a lot!"

And I do. I talk to God continuously. What is prayer finally but the art of talking and listening to God? It is not begging or bargaining. It is not magic or manipulation. It is presenting your naked self before the Almighty. It is to stand before God, stripped of title, degree, status, pomposity, and pretense to tell God how it is—and then to listen to God.

At times you experience such sheer joy that to contain it would of itself be blasphemy. At other times, of course, what you want to say is so overwhelmingly private or sacred that only God could or should hear it.

Life often presents you with circumstances that you are unable to control. Your intellect is insufficient; your articulation is mere babble; your resources are inadequate; your insights are blurred. In such moments, you discover through the power of prayer that God receives you in your ignorance, emptiness, blindness, pain, and brokenness.

Parents sometimes reach the end of their parental abilities. In spite of the best efforts, modeling, and counsel, offspring get sidetracked. You know not why, for you have apparently done all that a "perfect" parent is supposed to do. But you watch helplessly as a son or daughter clearly moves into a pattern of life that is inevitably destructive. And there is absolutely nothing you can do about it. You have already done all you can.

A couple tries desperately to hold together a marriage that is falling apart. Counseling does not help. Their best efforts and intentions are inadequate to restore a meaningful and lasting relationship.

A pastor struggles with a sermon. It simply will not come together. The commentaries are clear, but they do not help. She or he writes and writes, reads and reads, and nothing happens. The sermon doesn't materialize.

The illness is terminal. The latest medical procedures and medicines have run their course, but they cannot reverse or arrest the disease. Physicians can offer nothing more.

One day life looks utterly good. So many of your dreams have come to fruition; relationships are healthy; problems are manageable; challenges are purposeful.

At such times, you discover anew the value of prayer and your need to talk and listen to God. It is your special time with the Creator. Nothing else will suffice.

Prayer does not and should not take the place of communication with a close friend, family member, pastor, or professional counselor. To have such persons with whom you can confide is another of God's generous gifts, but these confidants cannot take the place of God. Prayer is the dimension reserved for you and God alone.

Prayer is the moment to be still, to listen, and to know that God is God. It is the context in which you regain perspective about yourself and circumstances. It is to shout or cry in the presence of God.

Prayer is cleansing, cathartic, and confrontive. Prayer is God's way of saying to us that we don't have to face life alone. No problem, no challenge, no joy, no concern is too big or too small for God's immediate attention.

FIRST AID FOR THE SOUL

After a while, the soul gets weary and needs tending. One should not allow the soul to go too long without attention—not the routine caring given to the soul, but the special tending when the traffic of life wearies the soul.

A weary soul becomes vulnerable to the wiles of evil, mischief, and sin. The attitude is damaged; the ability to withstand temptation is diminished. Irritability comes more readily. Un-Christian acts and unholy thoughts are evidences of the weary soul.

How do you tend your soul? Weekly worship is not sufficient for me; yet, how undernourished my soul and spirit would be without it. I need the power, comfort, support, and challenge of the community at worship. The preached Word, prayers, and people are sources of grounding. In the words of Antonio Salieri, Mozart's nemesis, music is "God's perfect language," and it lifts me beyond comprehension. But at times the soul cries out for more.

Schedules, expectations, demands, responsibilities, and frustrations have a way of finally taking their toll on us. Life becomes routine, mundane. Tasks become perfunctory, people incidental. We lose a sense of real caring. Sometimes depression sets in.

We must find ways of tending the soul, or our whole being grows stale. We will become hard or sour and spoiled. Jesus said, "You would become like salt that has lost its savor."

I must find a place, a time, sometimes a person for that special caring. I need to listen to silence and hear the soul's cries. Burdens are too heavy for weak shoulders to bear alone. There must be time to talk to God undisturbed and to listen.

There is something frightening and awe filled as the soul comes into the presence of God. The Old Testament calls it the "fear of God." Now I know what that means.

The soul is bare—no title, no status, no secrets—just naked in its weariness. There is no need to pretend or to impress. The soul is open to God's scrutiny and embrace. God comes as always because, in truth, God never leaves us. We only fail in our distractions to see God.

I write from my special place, surrounded by trees and the spirits of the saints. The quiet quiets me. The vastness forces me to keep perspective. The overwhelming presence of God assures me that I am not alone.

I hear the voice of God as surely as I hear the cries of God's people. Cries come from everywhere, but they no longer overwhelm me. In the midst of the cries, I hear God's voice: *"Go and do what you can, be*

*what I would have you be, and remember that I have
not forsaken you or left you alone."*

The soul has been tended once again in that special
way; it has been caressed and soothed. The body is
not so weary as before. The tears have been dried, the
hurts have been healed, the future has been made
more hopeful, love has been replenished.

READING FEEDS THE MIND
AND THE SOUL

I am an avid reader. At any one time, I'm reading a
half dozen books. They're lying throughout the house
with bookmark in place or opened or page corners
folded down. My desk always contains another stack
of books "to read." Reading is not only a professional
obligation and necessity, but also a way of exploring a
variety of worlds and stretching the mind.

By reading, I can go anywhere I desire. I can visit
South America or Egypt or Topeka. I can leave my
contemporary setting and visit another, such as
frontier America or eighteenth-century England.

What an unbelievable treasure is the mind. I
suppose God could have created us without the
capacity to think, reason, imagine, and argue. Instead
we were given the incredible capacity to reflect, to
ponder, to explore, and to create. Reading, for me,
has been one means by which I am able to be quiet and
to challenge myself as well as to expand my world and
deepen my faith.

During the Christmas holidays, I had several days
in which to relax. I enjoyed the family, watched birds

as they visited the feeder, watched football games (most of my teams lost!), and read.

Among my reading was *Ironweed* by William Kennedy, a novel set in Albany, New York. It so captivated my attention that I could not put it down. It is about "street people"—homeless wanderers who choose (or have no choice) to live an unconventional, unpredictable, and risk-filled existence. This is not a happy book. It easily depressed me, so I needed to read something else.

I discovered *Land Between the Rivers: The Southern Illinois Country* to be delightful, informative, and beautiful. I am told that many Illinois families have it in their homes.

I love history, so I thoroughly appreciated this history of southern Illinois. I learned the customs, resources, strengths, and beauty of this region. I also learned some of its not too proud history. This book did not win the Pulitzer Prize, as did *Ironweed,* but it has become one of my prized possessions. I know I will turn to this book again and again.

Reading ought to cause one to stretch and to argue. That's what happened when I began reading *On Liberation Theology,* edited by Ronald Nash. This is an interesting and provocative collection of well written articles by "ten distinguished conservative theologians and scholars." They provide a critical analysis of liberation theology. This was especially informative reading for me because, having read most of the proponents of liberation theology, I found it important to have a systematic, scholarly critique of this interpretation of the Christian faith.

I also began reading one of my favorite author's newest books, *In Search of Our Mothers' Gardens: Womanist Prose* by Alice Walker, a collection of articles, reflections, and prose by the author of *The Color Purple,* which was also awarded the Pulitzer Prize. When I make a speech, I often draw on insights from *The Color Purple* or Walker's *Their Eyes Were Watching God.*

In Search of Our Mothers' Gardens will make one sad, happy, and angry. It mostly made me proud. It shows the struggle to be fully human in the face of overwhelming odds.

As I moved in and out of these varied worlds, became involved in the struggles and lives of fictitious and real persons, evaluated the critique of scholars and theologians, absorbed the history and beauty of a part of my resident state, I knew that once again I had been visited by God.

Reading is not merely an intellectual exercise. It can be, and is for me, a holy moment.

TRUSTING GOD ON SLEEPLESS NIGHTS

I'm a long-time insomniac. For years, a full night's sleep has eluded me. It once was frustrating to lie in bed, tossing, wishing, and praying for sleep. I have come to terms with it now and have accommodated myself to fewer hours of sleep. I am up most mornings by four o'clock.

My colleagues over the years have ridiculed me for

my irregular sleeping patterns. The more irreverent ones have charged that I have a guilty conscience; the more pious ones have likened me to John Wesley, who rose between four and five o'clock each morning. As is the case in most of life, the truth is probably somewhere in between these extremes.

Recently, a member of the bishop's cabinet who was leading devotions focused his remarks on a meditation titled "Sleep" from a book called *God Speaks*. As he led us, other cabinet members began to chuckle. Finally, the district superintendent, realizing that I was the only one present who had sleeping problems, attempted to explain. I am still not sure if he was as innocent as he implored. His colleagues enjoyed his predicament.

Nevertheless the meditation was so meaningful that I requested a copy. I now carry it in my briefcase, read it periodically, and try to discern the ways in which it speaks to me. It is written in the first person, as if God were speaking. God reminds the reader that sleep is one of God's most precious gifts. It is, in fact, our "friend." God says that those who don't sleep well "lack confidence in me." This got my attention immediately!

The meditation continues to say that for those who work hard, the indictment is even stronger. God has especially provided rest, relaxation, and sleep for the weary body and spirit. Not to appropriate them is a "greater sin," because it is an indication that one does not trust God.

It is a moving and provocative word. Those who lie

awake worrying about past or current and future problems lose a sense of perspective. I imagine all of us talk about trusting God, then continue to operate our lives in a way that negates the claim. How many times have we taken a concern or problem to God, assured ourselves that it is in God's hands, then continued to worry about it? What does trust in God really mean?

I'm not one who wants to relinquish or avoid responsibility as a creature of God. Simply to drop things on God willy-nilly seems an expression of immature faith. I believe we have responsibility to use our minds, physical capacity, disciplined life, and our religious faith to help us grapple with life's struggles. But there comes a time when our human capacities reach their limitations. We can go no further. Exhausted, the soul and mind acknowledge that a greater source must now take the reins.

I trust God more than resolutions and treaties, governments and councils. I trust God more than creeds and logic. Yet, too many times, I do not "let go and let God," perhaps due to pride and the desire to be the master of my fate.

The meditation's thought is intriguing. Is a part of our restlessness, anxiety, fear, nervousness, and sleeplessness due to an inability to trust God? My mind already responds: It is not God in whom I lack trust and confidence, but someone in the human family. That's too easy, too obvious.

Life would have more meaning if we did utterly

trust God, not merely say we trust God and act as if our trust is elsewhere.

I believe God has a greater concern for the creation than I, that God cares more about us than we care about ourselves. I believe that God does not forget or forsake us.

When one has confidence and trust in God, what difference should it make? The meditation concludes with these words: "Blessed is he [and she] who hopes. And who sleeps."

FORGIVENESS: A HARD WORD TO LIVE UP TO

Forgiveness is difficult, even for a bishop! Forgiveness makes good sermon material or philosophical discussion, and it is often adorned with pious platitudes. We want forgiveness for ourselves but grudgingly give it to others.

One of the blessings of taking time from a busy day and hectic schedule for prayer, meditation, and reflection is that it provides an opportunity to look at your life before God—who and what you are or are not.

Some months ago, while at a "place apart," I found myself contemplating my life. In the quiet of that serene place, a long unsettled debt confronted me anew. It had plagued me for several years.

I had a friend at one time. We shared happy moments together—ministry, children, meals. We grew together. Then one day, unexpectedly, he said something that pained me greatly. He said it without malice. It came easily; he smiled when he said it. It seemed to me all too characteristically racist.

I tore into him verbally. He seemed stunned, then offended, soon defensive. One word led to another, and two friends were no more.

Now in my quiet moments with God, no quiet and peace existed. I could not have a "right" relationship with God while having a "wrong" relationship with a neighbor, friend, and colleague. I could not put it off any longer.

The note was short and to the point. I asked for forgiveness. I apologized. It made no difference who was at fault. Time has a way of making the important mundane. To my utter surprise, I received a four-page response from my friend. We needed to get this thing behind us. Ten years was a long time to carry a needless burden.

A few years ago I was a commencement speaker for a United Methodist school. A retired minister whom I did not know greeted me, then shocked me by asking forgiveness for holding a grudge against me since 1968. I had never seen the man. He had held me responsible for his failure to be elected to a particular office he desired. With tears, he said that he did more harm to his own spiritual life than to me. We shook hands, his apology was received, and I could tell immediately that he was a happier man.

I am struck by the number of broken relationships there are because no one wants to say, "I am sorry" or "I forgive you" or "Forgive me." Family members go for years without speaking to one another because of some spoken word or incident that brought pain. The wall, once erected, seems impossible to tear down. Frequently, the wall remains standing so long that the original cause is not remembered or in retrospect is not nearly so important as it seemed at the time.

Those who love each other deeply sometimes hurt each other the most. Without intending to inflict pain, it so easily is accomplished. Yet other times we go for the jugular, knowing and hoping that our words or actions will devastate. Afterwards, in the light of reason, in the clarity of time, the decent within us reveals that what we said and did was not the highest standard that we know. The awesome need of ego will not permit those reconciling words to be spoken—"I am sorry, forgive me" or "I forgive you." The words don't come easily.

Jesus constantly reminded his followers that their love for one another determined the validity of their love for him. As we would want to be forgiven, we must also forgive. Such is integral to being a faithful disciple.

Is there someone who needs to hear those words from you, someone who hurt you or someone you hurt? Pick up the phone, write the note, or take the person by the hand and simply say those reconciling words.

You have no assurance that they will be received, but an inner peace and strength will come to you when you attempt to bring unity where there is division, healing where there is brokenness. On the other hand, you may be pleasantly surprised to learn how

The Spring of Personal Discipline ||| 37

welcome your words will be to the one who wanted to say them, but lacked the inner resource to do so. Now you have made the difference.

I waited ten years to say, "I am sorry." That's much too long. But forgiveness is difficult, even for a bishop.

MARRIAGE AND THE CHRISTIAN COMMITMENT

Some weeks ago, I wrote a letter of congratulations to a pastor and spouse on the occasion of their fiftieth wedding anniversary, celebrated on Christmas Day. During the year, I have written several of such letters. In a day when the institution of marriage seems fragile, it is important to affirm and celebrate those marriages that endure.

Of all human relationships, marriage is the most challenging and, perhaps, the most satisfying in its unique way. It demands commitment, love, flexibility, and a high degree of unselfishness.

In some ways, marriage demands too much of its partners. Each is expected to fulfill a variety of needs for the other that no one person can or ought to be expected to fulfill. While marriage can be good, it can also be tough. On every marriage certificate should be stamped, "Toughness and tenderness required."

Marriage has been under siege the last few years. Many young people, having lived in homes in which they saw unhappy marriages, have opted not to marry at all. "Why put yourself through the hassle?" they ask.

Others are afraid of commitment and choose simply to keep their options available. Some reason that the "higher" form of commitment is not to commit yourself in marriage. That logic confuses me.

The United States has one of the highest divorce rates in the world. This may be true in part because of the growing tendency to emphasize pleasure over commitment. We live in a "disposable" society: If something breaks, throw it out; if it causes you problems, get another one; when it ceases to make you feel good, switch to another brand. A sense of permanence and commitment is becoming obsolete.

The United Methodist Church's Social Principles affirm the following:

> *Marriage.*—We affirm the sanctity of the marriage covenant which is expressed in love, mutual support, personal commitment, and shared fidelity between a man and a woman. . . .
> *Divorce.*—Where marriage partners, even after thoughtful consideration and counsel, are estranged beyond reconciliation, we recognize divorce as regrettable but recognize the right of divorced persons to remarry. . . .
> *Single persons.*—We affirm the integrity of single persons, and we reject all social practices that discriminate or social attitudes that are prejudicial against persons because they are unmarried. (*Discipline,* par. 71 *C-E*)

These positions held by the church are reasonable and sensible. They express the kind of commitment and compassion that should reflect the nature of the Christian community. Not everyone should marry.

Not everyone should be married to the person to whom he or she is married. Not everyone should remain married. Not every marriage that breaks down should be dissolved.

Marriage is a gift from God, and those who accept it must work diligently to keep it alive and vibrant. I am a strong supporter of marriage enrichment programs that seek to help couples make marriage a richer experience. At the same time, I firmly believe that when the relationship begins to break down, couples should seek to fix it immediately. When they recognize that what is needed is beyond their capacity to give, they should seek pastoral and other professional assistance. No stone should be left unturned to try to restore and maintain the marriage relationship.

Yet there are those times when marriage partners are estranged beyond reconciliation, and to remain in marriage is more destructive than terminating it would be. Indeed, divorce or separation may be the more redemptive response.

The church has a responsibility as a nurturing, caring, correcting community to embrace all members of the community. It must never, even inadvertently, suggest that a person's value is dependent on his or her marital status. One is not more or less valuable because he or she is married, divorced, or single; all are precious in the sight of God.

What is expected of all members in the Christian community is that they express and reflect the love of

Christ in all their relationships and be true to the highest values of the Christian faith.

We are important to God not because we are single, married, or divorced, but because we are God's.

ARE YOU LISTENING TODAY?

My twelve-year-old daughter sat on the floor. I was reading the newspaper in solitude when her words screamed out at me: "Daddy, you always do that!"

I was surprised, astonished. This was my soft-spoken, somewhat shy, youngest daughter, my "baby."

As I looked up from my paper, I saw such hurt in her eyes that I hurt, too, without knowing the details. Her next words devastated me.

"Daddy, you don't listen to me when I talk to you!"

In an instant, the place within, that reservoir where tears are stored, wanted to erupt; I had to stop it immediately. Now I had more hurt in my eyes than she in hers.

Her little face changed, her expression softened. She somehow knew that not only had she gotten my attention, but also that much more had taken place between this father and daughter.

I said, "I'm very sorry, and if you ever feel that I'm not listening to you, tell me." I gave her a kiss, but we both had given each other much more.

The guilt level rose in me, however. I have prided myself on my ability to listen. I listen to everyone, hear everyone's complaints, concerns, problems, dreams, and joys. How long had I not been listening to my daughter—two weeks, two months, two years, more? It saddened me greatly.

She did not say, as she will no doubt as she enters those teen years, "Daddy, you're not hearing me!" I have discovered that the translation of that phrase is, "You don't agree with me."

What my daughter was saying was far more profound and incriminating: "You won't listen to my words." Indeed, she was saying what I consider to be a great travesty in human relationships, "You are ignoring me." To ignore another human being is unconscionable.

I have attended workshops called "listening labs." There you spend a lot of time and money for someone to tell you how to listen. I have read book after book on human interaction and been in more dialogue groups than I can count. But I failed the test with my daughter, with whom I should have been most proficient.

A singing group made famous a song with these words, "You always hurt the one you love, the one you shouldn't hurt at all." That melody clamored in my head that day. I did not want to hurt my twelve-year-old daughter.

Listening to one another is essential to communication, to understanding, and to meaningful relationships. Many problems are accentuated because some group or individual feels ignored. One can accept being disagreed with and argued with, but not being ignored. People want to be acknowledged, to be taken seriously—old people, young people, children, all people.

Some play a game at listening. They give the appearance of listening when the mind is elsewhere. Others half listen, hearing enough to contribute minimally to conversation. Still others listen begrudgingly only long enough to get their opportunity to have "their say." Some, like "professional listeners," are skilled at listening to counselees, clients, employees, and parishioners, but are poor listeners at home.

To listen is "to attend closely as to hear." To do that requires ear and heart and mind. Is there someone you should be listening to—adversary, colleague, loved one, God?

ACKNOWLEDGING SIN AND GIVING IT TO GOD

I was surprised by a headline in the *New York Times,* "Pope says sin 'lies with individuals.' " The article appeared, not in the Sunday religious section, but in the front section, where it would receive immediate attention. I did not expect to see an article about sin in a leading newspaper. In fact, we seldom use the word *sin* anymore.

The occasion for the article was the issuance of a document on sin and penance by Pope John Paul II, entitled "Reconciliatio et Paenitentia" or "Reconciliation and Penance." While I have not read it in full, I thoroughly agree with a portion of the statement. The *New York Times* reports, "In the document, the Pope repeatedly emphasized individual responsibility and warned that modern societies had so diluted the concept of personal sin that they no longer held individuals accountable for their actions."

In the holy season of Lent, we are called to an awareness of our personal and private sin. Sin is a reality of our human predicament. No one escapes it. None dare say they have no need of forgiveness and penance. Each of us must acknowledge our individual failings, those times when we fall short of the glory God intended for us.

To admit our personal and private sin is to acknowledge our free will, a gift of God. To acknowledge our free will is to recognize our personal responsibility.

The failure to accept personal responsibility for sin and transferring it to society or institutions produces more of a problem than a cure. Pope John Paul II says, "This usage contrasts social sin and personal sin, not without ambiguity, in a way that leads more or less unconsciously to the watering down and almost abolition of personal sin, with the recognition only of social guilt and responsibility."

Let me say at once that I do believe in social sin and social guilt. I have just begun reading Samuel Pisar's *Of Blood and Hope*. It is a powerful and painful description of the experience of being a Jew in Europe under the reign of Nazism. How can one know of Auschwitz or the Gulag or South Africa and not believe in social sin?

The point, however, is not to dismiss the reality of social sin—the collective transgressions of people, manifested in institutional sanctions and systemic injustice—but to accept the profundity of personal sin.

In 1973, the noted physician and psychiatrist Dr. Karl Menninger, founder of the world famous Menninger Clinic, wrote a helpful book with the intriguing title *What Ever Became of Sin?* He points out what can and does happen to us when we fail to take into account the "ought" of life, the "thou shalt nots" of life. We blame systems, organizations, or others for our failure. When all constraints are done away with, when we are without an overarching sense of wrong, then it is not long before the sense of sin is lost. As Dr. Menninger points out, even the use of the term disappears from our vocabulary.

As a former sociology major in college, I have known and accepted the influence that environment plays on our behavior and attitude. I know full well the weight of social sin and the relationship of society in individual behavior. Yet, I believe strongly in the concepts of free will, individual responsibility, and grace.

When I was a boy, a saying used frequently by the elders of the community was, "If you make your bed hard, you will have to lie in it." I was taught early to accept responsibility for my misdeeds. I was punished more severely if I lied about a misdeed than when I confessed my failure or fault. It was a good lesson.

A part of being human is to recognize our shortcomings. Who is perfect? None among us. We cannot fully know God's grace until we sense personally how little we deserve it.

What better time to reflect on our sinful nature than Lent? Most people like to confess the sins of their neighbors, but this is a time to confess your sins, your acts of failure to do that which is pleasing to God. That you are a sinner is no disgrace, but that you fail to acknowledge your sin is an act of unfaithfulness. The Christ who redeems is also the Christ who forgives and makes new.

Urban P. Holmes III, in *Spirituality for Ministry*, says, "American religion is obsessed with the 'warm sins' "—sins of the flesh, such as drunkenness and sexual promiscuity. Those are real enough, but they hardly exhaust the ways we displease God. Militarism, sexism, ethnocentrism, prejudice, racism, classism, greed, selfishness, envy, and pride—all are equally sinful in God's sight.

Take time during the season of Lent to examine your sin. Own it; accept responsibility for it. Don't make excuses or rationalizations. Don't call it by sophisticated sociological or psychological jargon. Call it by its name. God already knows it. God wants you to claim it, to acknowledge it. Then with a penitent and contrite heart, give it to God. Leave it with God. There is no sin so terrible that God's love cannot forgive.

BEING SENSITIVE TO ONE ANOTHER

Shortly before Christmas, he slipped and now finds himself with a "handicapping condition." He is now walking with crutches and is in a cast from his hip down. A day or two following the accident, my colleague said, "You surely get sensitized in a hurry!"

Now he is much more aware of the value of buildings with ramps and a minimum of steps, the convenience and necessity of parking spaces set aside for those with disabilities and handicapping conditions, and the insensitivity of those more able-bodied, who park in those places because they are too lazy or inconsiderate to walk a few extra yards.

I am also more sensitized.

A few years ago, Howard Griffin, a white Southerner, determined to become "black" through a skin dye, ultra violet rays, and a series of pills that would darken his skin. He so altered his appearance that no one could detect that he was actually white. He planned to follow an itinerary, first as a black man, then he would retrace his journey as a white man.

He walked the same streets, went to the same stores, encountered most of the same people. He recorded the incredible difference in the treatment he received in a fascinating book titled *Black Like Me*. It was an instructive experiment. He became sensitized!

One cannot be expected to go to such extremes to understand the plight and experiences of others, especially those who hurt. Yet, it is not unreasonable to expect that people will care enough to try to understand.

Those with physical disabilities are increasingly being "mainstreamed." No longer are they kept hidden or separated from those in society who don't have severe physical disabilities.

They are now in the work place, classroom, malls, and, it is hoped, in our churches. They want not so much sympathy as sensitivity to our language in describing "them," to our actions toward "them," and to the provisions for buildings and a multitude of conveniences and necessities that those without such conditions take for granted. All of us, whatever our gender, race, status, or condition in life, desire that others should treat us with respect, caring, and understanding as a part of the human family.

One definition of *sensitive* that I especially like is "keen in sensibility." It is to be sharp in one's awareness of others, to know at once what is appropriate or inappropriate, to know what immediately makes one feel included and what isolates, what hurts and what heals. To have keen sensibilities is what we need one for the other, to understand and to empathize with others, as a part of mature and responsible living. It is what is meant by *koinonia*— the Christian community.

Out of our sensitivity should flow altered behavior, for to be sensitive without changed actions is not to be sensitive at all.

There is and ought to be a connectedness of the human family that enables us to be joined inseparably to one another. One of Alice Walker's characters in *The Color Purple* declares that sometimes she feels so connected to her environment that if she were to cut down a tree, her arm would bleed. That's sensitivity!

The words of the familiar hymn speak eloquently to this need:

We share each other's woes,
Our mutual burdens bear,
And often for each other flows
The sympathizing tear.
                    ("Blest Be the Tie That Binds")

THE SUMMER OF
FREEDOM AND JUSTICE

*The new world is a world of geographical togetherness.
This means that no individual or nation can live alone. . . .
Through our scientific genius we have made of the world a
neighborhood; now through our moral and spiritual genius
we must make of it a brotherhood. We are all involved in the
single process. Whatever affects one directly affects all
indirectly. We are all links in the great chain of humanity.*

*A . . . challenge that stands before us is that of entering the
new age with understanding good will. This simply means
that the Christian virtues of love, mercy, and forgiveness
should stand at the center of our lives.*

—Martin Luther King, Jr.
Address: *Facing the Challenge of
a New Age*

PARADES AND FLAGS AND
THE AMERICAN IDEAL

I have never been "big" on patriotism, but have always been patriotic. It would be difficult to grow up in New York City and not be patriotic; we had parades for every occasion and for almost every group.

The flags and music of our country have long been a part of my experience. The words were meaningful even when I learned they did not then apply to me. Justice, freedom, liberty—noble concepts. As a boy, I knew the intent was right, although the application was not universal to all citizens.

The literature, poetry, and music of America spoke to that region of my yearnings that so wanted to be free and to belong. I learned the Preamble to the Constitution with pride, as did many a school boy and girl. I recited by memory the Gettysburg Address. I wanted to be a good citizen, proud of my country, but it was difficult. So much of my experience was dilemma and paradox.

When I wanted to love my country, I was certain my country did not love me. Yet the American ideal would not let go. At its best, it is unmatched. I decided to hold onto the ideal even when the performance of the government and the attitude of its citizens were contrary to it.

On Independence Day, I remember that ideal, not the imperfections of leaders, not our checkered history or contemporary vagaries. I remember many words about country, God, citizenship, and freedom. I ask God to bless America because without God's blessing and guidance, we wander off course. We forget our own principles. I sing "America, the Beautiful" and remember the right, the beauty, and the goodness in our land.

I see our flag and remember the justice for which it stands—not domination, materialism, or colonialism. I look beyond the years to the fulfillment of noble goals our forebears strived for. I know I must expand the dreams and enlarge the vision beyond that of the "founding fathers." I must see justice for all those the founders did not see.

On Independence Day, while enjoying parades, music, and family gatherings, I picture the nation at its best, holding forever what we can be, remembering our finest hours. I get a lump in my throat when the music of my nation is played.

One nation under God—I like that. It sounds right. To some, it is sentimental and trite, to others it is perfunctory language without substance. But I believe it. Every nation is under God, acknowledged or not.

On Independence Day, I rededicate myself to country—not to blind patriotism, but to be doggedly patriotic, to chastise my nation and leaders when they forget the ideal for which we stand, to confront, engage, and embrace this nation of such utter diversity, great capacity, and unrealized potential.

I pray for my nation and its citizens and will not be content until every citizen feels a sense of belonging and caring by the country. I pray for my government and its policies so that the ideals of justice for all are applied to our dealings with other nations. I will work toward the election of leaders who demonstrate that this is their dream for a greater America.

On Independence Day, I remember with deep gratitude that I live in a nation in which I can pen my thoughts freely and without threat of governmental reprisal, and I will give myself to ensure this right for all. I will resist any effort by anyone, including the government, to abridge the fundamental rights of its citizens.

This nation under God means something special to me. On Independence Day, I am reminded of its significance.

GOD'S FAMILY IS EVERYWHERE

In Stockholm, Sweden, it is a beautiful Sunday morning. This city of trees, water, and rocks is glistening. Composed of fourteen islands, the city has water everywhere.

This day is especially quiet. It is the third and final day of the Swedish holiday "Mid-summer's Night," which commemorates the coming of summer and is marked by twenty-four hours of daylight. The

Swedish take the holiday seriously and literally empty the city, going to the countryside and visiting one or more of the sixty-nine thousand lakes in this picturesque country. There is little movement here this morning.

While I am here, thousands of miles away, I feel very much at home on this Sabbath morning. Birds sing a familiar carol. Trees, in brilliant green, bend in the morning wind as they do in Illinois. The sky is as blue, clouds as fluffy and white, and the quiet morning is a friend to me.

My favorite Psalm is 139. The psalmist describes the omnipresence of God. Where can one go and not be in the presence of God? To the heavens—no! To the uttermost parts of the sea—no! Not even in Sweden or Finland or the Soviet Union. There is no place one can go and be outside the care and presence of God.

I am aware of the presence of God in this setting that some would describe as a "foreign" country. It is my first visit here, and I am unfamiliar with the language, customs, and traditions, but it is not a foreign place to me.

When I set my feet on this soil for the first time, God was here to welcome me. Wherever God is, I cannot call that place foreign. I sense God's presence all about me. The more pronounced the presence of God, the less I feel a stranger.

The nearness of God this Lord's day is as real as I have sensed anywhere. At times, God's presence is so evident that I must speak audibly to God; to speak silently is insufficient. I must hear my words spoken, for God is as near as any human being occupying the same room. It is sometimes embarrassing, but now my wife, Kim, is at least used to it. I try to find a quiet room so that I cannot be accused of being some kind of eccentric.

Today, here in Stockholm, God is so close one must speak not only with the mind but also with the mouth. Are there not times when you feel that you could reach out and touch God?

To worship God in a new and different setting is to understand anew a dimension of God and a character of the human family. One does not need to go to a particular place or land or setting to find God. In the ultimate sense, all ground is holy, made so by the presence of God.

God's family, too, is everywhere, not just in the United States or one part of it. The whole human family is God's creation. Wherever one goes, one is met by family members. The family is not just those who speak the same language, bear the same color, or claim the same nation.

In a few days, I will leave Sweden for the Soviet Union. How reassuring it is to know that even where God is officially denied, the reality of God will be no less real. *God is! God is present!* Nowhere can one escape the presence of God and the family of God.

A PRIME CANDIDATE FOR CHRIST'S AMAZING GRACE

Bitburg! It has brought back many memories. President Ronald Reagan's controversial trip to this

German community and its cemetery stirred the emotions of many. I read the editorials, listened to the arguments, heard again the pain of those who suffered so much at the hands of Nazism. Bitburg brought back childhood memories as well.

I remember air raid shelters and the respected air raid warden with white helmet and arm band. I remember rationing stamps and dark green window shades, called "blackout" shades. I recall blackouts, hearing sirens go off when one least expected them. All lights would go out; New York City would become dark in a matter of seconds. For us, it was a drill. For others, all over Europe, it was reality.

I remember my relatives, handsome in army uniform, but absent, as were fathers, sons, husbands, sisters, and daughters of other families.

I remember a horrible screech one afternoon that resounded throughout the apartment building. The telegram had arrived, informing a neighbor that her loved one had been "killed in action."

Bitburg brought it all back to me.

As a mere lad, I would go each Saturday to our local movie theater to get a close-up of the war via Hollywood. I would see the Nazi soldiers with their goose steps, sinister looks, and heavy accents. The character of Adolph Hitler was the personification of evil. I did not realize the depths of such evil.

I remember overhearing debates about how wrong it was for black soldiers (then we were called "Negro") to fight a war in Europe when neither they nor their children enjoyed many of the freedoms they were fighting to preserve. I was learning a valuable lesson about the ambiguity of life, a lesson that serves me yet today.

Bitburg and the discussion of World War II have caused me to reflect on one who has greatly influenced my own thought and faith, Dietrich Bonhoeffer. He was executed on April 9, 1945, in Slossenberg, Germany.

Bonhoeffer, a son of Germany, resisted Hitler and all for which that government stood. Preacher, teacher, theologian, he risked his life because his faith would not let him participate in nor cooperate with the tyranny, racism, and depravity that were World War II Germany.

Bitburg has caused me to think about the meaning of grace and sin. I see in it no political statement, no political act. I am forced to face the reality of ambiguity. "While we were yet sinners, Christ died for us."

Bitburg, West Germany; Auschwitz, Poland; Johannesburg, South Africa; Philadelphia, Mississippi; Montgomery, Alabama—the list could go on and embrace every continent. These places are reminders of the depth to which the human soul can sink. Those who are perpetrators of such heinous acts are prime candidates for Christ's "amazing grace." This is no political statement but a theological one, promise of a loving God, one whose cosmic economy is so different from that to which we are accustomed.

I have no idea what President Reagan said as he stood amid the dead at Bitburg. I clearly do not know what he expected from his visit. But my soul grieves for those who lie there, those who gave their lives for such an unworthy cause—racism and Nazism. I want to denounce such travesties so loudly and clearly that wherever their expressions are found today, and in whatever form, the world will never forget what hatred can do to the hater as well as to the hated.

Bitburg is a reminder of all those who suffer because they are different, but especially those who paid the ultimate price, life itself, in the Holocaust—women, men, and children slaughtered, tortured, experimented on, humiliated.

I remember those men and women of all ages who give themselves to causes and philosophies whose purpose is to oppress, suppress, dehumanize, exploit, and abuse members of the human family. I pray for them in life and in death. My spirit longs to forgive even when my mind finds it difficult to do so.

Bitburg. It is a painful reminder of sin and depravity. Yet nowhere is God's grace more needed.

THE HUMAN QUESTION OF BEING A VICTIM

It began with Adam—"the victim syndrome" or the need to blame others for our failures. It is characterized by our refusal to take responsibility for our actions. Some predetermined force or factors become the reasons for our behavior.

I am such a firm believer in free will that I resist

most deterministic explanations, sociological and theological, that appear to limit individual freedom and responsibility. Such a view makes my life considerably more difficult; it is easier to go through life as victim.

Certainly, victims exist; they are everywhere. However, not everyone who claims to be a victim is one, and victims are not victims in every situation.

In a society so shaped by racism, one who is born to the "out" or "inferior" race faces a life challenge: How does one discern the difference between being the victim and the failure to assume individual responsibility for one's attitude and behavior? This was a challenge to my parents, and it is to Kim and me. How do we enable our daughters to live, not as victims, but as victims who will not live as victims? This issue relates not only to race or gender or class, but is also an age-old question that confronts the entire human family.

Too many people have the need to blame others—even God—for their misfortune and lack of courage, character, or achievement. Indeed, if you are a member of some of the obvious "victim categories"—poor in a class society, female in a male-dominated one, or non-white in a white society—the greater is the temptation to conclude that all of life deals with you on the basis of your victim category and that you deal with life always from your context as a victim. It is a struggle!

I do not minimize the socialization process through which we all pass, but sooner or later we must stop blaming others for our actions. The moment comes when each individual must claim her or his own responsibility. One's sexist behavior, for instance, cannot forever be blamed on one's grandfather.

That there is evil in the world, none would deny, but I am not at all in agreement with the claim that, "The devil made me do it!"

William Sloane Coffin, the dynamic minister of the historic Riverside Church in New York City, is one of my favorite preachers. I was shocked some time ago when I learned of his son's tragic death at the age of twenty-four. In his book *The Courage to Love,* Dr. Coffin included a sermon he preached on the occasion of his son's death. It is a moving testimony of a father's grief and a Christian's faith.

When a well-intentioned neighbor implied that it was God's will that young Coffin's car should leave the road that dark, wintry night and land in Boston Harbor, Bill Coffin immediately responded. He would not let God be blamed for the absence of a guard rail or street lights or for young Alex's failure to get the windshield wipers fixed, perhaps his driving too fast in that terrible storm, or perhaps his having had "one too many." No! He would not let God be blamed. That takes character.

Increasingly, it appears that no perpetrator of a crime, however heinous, takes responsibility. The husband beats his wife to death, a mother her child; a man rapes a woman as she enters her apartment, a group shoots a young man because his girlfriend is the wrong color. All claim to be innocent—not guilty, not responsible for their actions. I wonder how long they went through life absolving themselves.

One of life's oldest deceptions convinces us that we are always victims. I remember well the day I realized that some people did not like me because of *who* I was and not *what* I was. They would not like me whatever my color. I began to see myself beyond a "victim category." I had to assume responsibility for my behavior. I could no longer summarily conclude that all reactions to me were based on my "victim category." It forced me to scrutinize carefully attitudes and actions and to try to distinguish between circumstances and conditions over which I had no control and those for which I alone must assume responsibility. It was both a freeing and an over-whelming realization.

The next time you are prepared to blame some-one—spouse, parent, child, friend, minister, institution, government, or society—for situations or circumstances in which you find yourself, dare to stop for a moment and ask, "Lord, is it I?"

MORAL DECISIONS AMID COMPLEX ISSUES

Life is filled with contradictions. Old clichés do not work anymore, if they ever did. Good people do suffer, and the wicked do prosper. And right, at least in one's lifetime, does not always triumph.

Issues are not nearly as simple as they are sometimes described. Take the matter of life—all would agree that it is sacred . . . but! I find it interesting that often those who oppose "freedom of choice" on the abortion issue tend to favor capital punishment; those who oppose capital punishment tend to favor abortion. Both groups use the same argument, the sanctity of life, to support their positions for preserving life.

I have observed with considerable interest some of the leaders in the forefront of the legitimate fight against pornography. Many of these "leaders" stand at the rear of the fight against bigotry and racism, which are every bit as destructive and obscene and which daily dehumanize men, women, and children.

Governments display the same kind of inconsistency. The morality of an issue is judged on the basis of whether it is perceived to be in the best national interest. It has been said that the difference between a freedom fighter and a terrorist depends on which side you support.

I worry when the church or church leaders begin to think that the morality of a situation is determined by who is doing it or saying it. One group speaks against its government and is considered a brave dissenter; another group does the same and is labeled traitor. The Left seems to have one set of morals for its friends, the Right another set. How can one favor free speech, even to the extent of criticizing the government, for one group of people and not for another?

I do not like dictatorships. It makes no difference to me whether they are socialist, capitalist, Marxist, or Christian—evangelical, conservative, or liberal. The right of free speech and dissent must be preserved for all people no matter what the political system in which they find themselves.

A prominent author caught in the hysteria of the McCarthy era in the 1950s was summoned before the House Un-American Activities Committee. Considerable effort was exerted to persuade her to reveal information that she believed was protected as a constitutional right. This hearing violated her strict sense of ethics. She said at one point during her ordeal, "I refuse to shape my morality to fit this year's fashions." She paid dearly!

A few weeks ago, I had breakfast with a prominent national politician; I believe his colleagues would agree that he is a man of superior character. Following breakfast, his aide gave me a copy of the politician's latest book. It is interesting and insightful, but I feel that those of the opposite political party would have difficulty with much of it. The book is not so much about partisan politics as it is about morality and the challenge faced by those who must make difficult and complex moral decisions.

The book opens with the author's contention "that there are morally preferred options and that it is the responsibility of humanity and of government to strive toward the good no matter how erratic and tortuous the path may be." That came from a politician, not a bishop!

Every solution faced in life will not be nearly so simple; sometimes we must choose between two or three unfavorable options. At other times, our choices will mean unpopularity among our friends and rejection by peers and even family members. There are also those occasions when, as my politician friend writes, "our moral stance brings about an immoral result."

The Christian, like all others, faces complex moral decisions. Answers are not easy, simple, or clearcut, as illustrated by the fact that Christians are found on both sides of issues, such as Nicaragua, racism, abortion, war, the arms race, the nation's budget, homosexuality, and so on.

My friend is right. There are morally preferred options, and our task is to find them, to choose them, and then to "strive toward the good, no matter how erratic and tortuous that path may be."

WOMEN'S JOURNEYS IN ALL AGES

I wanted to see the monument. I had read about it, but I wanted to see it up close. I touched the base, read the inscriptions, looked up, but was too close to get a good view.

I stepped back into the street. The view was marvelous! I wanted to climb on it as I had climbed on monuments as a boy in New York City.

The place was the town square of Vandalia, only a few yards from the grand old building that once was the state capitol of Illinois. The height of the monument surprised me. Its beauty was moving. Suddenly, I wanted to cry; I knew I would do it later.

I was examining, touching, admiring the "Madonna of the Trail," a magnificent statue commemorating "pioneer mothers." One inscription at its base reads in bold print: MEMORIAL PIONEER MOTHERS COVERED WAGON DAYS.

She stands tall, strong, almost defiant. Long legs, strong body, tough features, firm hands. A little boy clutches her thigh as if it were a difficult task, for the mother seems to be moving at a fast pace, and in her arms is another child. Her eyes look straight ahead, determined, purposeful.

I thought about pioneer mothers and daughters, not only those who came on covered wagons with families and husbands to settle the state of Illinois, but also those whose pioneering efforts have never been memorialized in granite or stone or marble.

They have been present in every age, of every race, color, and creed. They dared to move in places forbidden to them. They had to be mother, wife, homemaker, provider, and confidante. The social milieu discouraged any expression of their talents other than prescribed "womanly" roles.

The history of the treatment of mothers, daughters, and sisters of the race and faith is at least contradictory. On the one hand, they were protected and idolized. On the other, they were objectified and suppressed. Rarely were the actions out of a sense of disdain; it was, rather, taken for granted that men should be men and women should be women. There were clear, even divinely defined, roles for both.

The "trail" has been a long one; the journey has not yet ended. There are frontiers yet to be blazed. Too many among us are not fully sensitized; we still do not see mothers, wives, sisters, and daughters of the race and faith as whole persons. Some cannot see beyond gender, which is a given but is only a part of what makes a human being.

Our language often reflects our insensitivity. No harm is intended, but harm is done when we ignore or stereotype by ill chosen words.

Many still believe that one's innate worth is determined by one's gender. They know ahead of time that female physicians, certified public accountants, welders, pastors, bishops, or pilots can never be equal to men in those positions.

I thank God for change. We experience it with joy and, sometimes, anxiety. When I stood before the statue on that grey, dreary morning, I thought about the women pioneers and how much we owe them.

I remember with gratitude those laywomen and clergywomen of the faith who have been pioneers in the church. They have entered the frontiers of the faith, those facets of our organizational and ecclesiastical life marked for centuries, "Men Only."

I thank God for the "Madonnas of the Trail":

—who sacrificed so that their children would have opportunities denied them, those who deferred or gave up careers so that a husband, sister, son, daughter, or brother could pursue one;

—who, as clergy, have experienced loneliness, isolation, and prejudice, and have given quality ministry where there was little support or encouragement;

—who have pioneered in a vast array of professions

and careers, thereby enriching our lives and broadening our human resources;

—who experienced, and still experience, physical, emotional, and psychological abuse. May we be more sensitive to their plight and provide a ministry that is healing and compassionate;

—whose faces vividly come to mind and those whom I will never see or know, those on farms and in villages and towns and cities, those of every size and shape, color and tongue, of great and modest intellect, those who "wait tables," type letters, and clean homes and offices.

I remember with profound appreciation and gratitude the "Madonnas of the Trail." I am overwhelmed by their sacrifice and their gifts, their grace and endurance, and their capacity to love and forgive.

I want to cry. Now is a good time.

THE CHURCH, WHICH GAVE BIRTH TO KING'S MOVEMENT, MUST CARRY IT ON

My wife, Kim, and I were attending the annual Martin Luther King, Jr., Memorial Breakfast on the birth date of the slain leader, January 15, now the first national holiday to honor a black American. The thousand people present in four degree weather came from all walks of life. I was moved to tears as I sat observing, remembering, hoping.

Reminiscent of the throngs who gathered during the Civil Rights era, they came from all over

Springfield, Illinois, and surrounding areas—black, white, professionals, clerks, wealthy, those not so financially secure. The politicians were there as were Protestants, Catholics, and Jews; we were all together. There are not many gatherings like this anymore. I sat next to a rabbi and he next to a priest. We chatted; we remembered.

Martin Luther King, Jr., short of stature, was a giant. He preached an uncompromising message of Christian love and non-violent resistance. He believed fervently in the family of God. He challenged us and changed us. In the end, he lost his life. I'm sure God cried.

I recently heard a moving sermon by one of our pastors on the "unconverted areas" of our lives. We all have them. For many in our nation, and I suppose in our church, one of those unconverted areas is our attitude toward and treatment of others whose race or ethnic background is different from ours. Many people suffer tragically because of these "unconverted areas" of their lives.

Dr. King endeavored to help a whole nation look at this unconverted area of its national life. He confronted us all, the church and the individual. It was, and still is, painful.

In the program booklet distributed at the memorial breakfast was printed the full text of the classic, "Letter from Birmingham City Jail." It is a letter written on April 16, 1963, to the clergy of Birmingham, Alabama, who criticized Dr. King for his efforts to abolish the oppressive system of segregation under which citizens were forced to live in that city.

Dr. King's letter is one of the most moving you will ever read. I read it again that morning.

Many do not remember those days. Others of us have it so indelibly etched on our souls we can never forget. What I remember so well about our efforts in those days was the spiritual character of our struggle. We met in the church, planned in the church, cried in the church, and celebrated in the church. There were times of great preaching and inspirational singing. Martin insisted that our struggle was a moral one and had to be undergirded by our faith in the gospel.

Before one could participate in the demonstrations, especially in the "sit-ins," one had to commit oneself to a set of principles called "Ten Commandments of the Non-Violent Movement." The movement was a product of churches, and the first participants were recruited from them.

Ten Commandments

I hereby pledge myself, my person, and my body, to the Non-Violent Movement. Therefore, I will keep the following Ten Commandments:

1. Meditate daily on the teachings and life of Jesus.
2. Remember always that the non-violent movement in Birmingham seeks justice and reconciliation—not victory.
3. Walk and talk in the manner of love, for God is love.
4. Pray daily to be used by God in order that all men might be free.

5. Sacrifice personal wishes in order that all men might be free.

6. Observe with both friend and foe the ordinary rules of courtesy.

7. Seek to perform regular service for others and for the world.

8. Refrain from the violence of fist, tongue, or heart.

9. Strive to be in good spiritual and bodily health.

10. Follow the directions of the movement and of the captain on a demonstration.

I would that our contemporary activists, liberal and conservative, so ordered their movement and activities. Groups today are too mean-spirited.

I thank God that we have made progress in some of those "unconverted areas" of our national and personal life, thanks in large measure to the life and ministry of Dr. King. However, there is much yet to be done before we can be satisfied.

Dr. King's birthday offers an opportunity to remember with thanksgiving the progress we have made and those who have sacrificed their lives for that progress.

Perhaps your congregation or community does not utilize this occasion for such remembrances and thanksgiving. If not, I invite you to consider calling together key leaders in the congregations and community to begin plans for next year. Make it a community-wide event, interfaith and interracial if possible. If that cannot be done, consider having an ecumenical event. Let this be a time of recommitment to the goals of racial justice and inclusiveness.

The closing lines of Dr. King's letter, written twenty-five years ago, are:

> Let us all hope that the dark clouds of racial prejudice will soon pass away and the deep fog of misunderstanding will be lifted from our fear-drenched communities and in some not too distant tomorrow the radiant stars of love and brotherhood will shine over our great nation with all their scintillating beauty.

I still have that dream!

A RESURGENCE OF RACISM WILL THWART INCLUSIVE CHURCH AND SOCIETY

I had not been called "nigger" within hearing distance in years. The two boys on bicycles were enjoying a warm spring day. They were typical, all-American boys—good lads, I'm sure, perhaps even United Methodists. The one speaking, perhaps, didn't intend that we hear the epithet; he was chided by his playmate not to say "that" word, at least not so we could hear it. I don't think my twelve-year-old daughter heard it; at least she didn't react. My wife did.

The whole affair passed quickly. We had more important matters to attend to, and we had long ago learned not to let such mindless remarks mar a beautiful day. But I have thought about it since the incident occurred.

It is important to keep such incidents in perspective, not giving them too much attention or too little. In our family's day-to-day experience, such naked expressions of racism and bigotry are rare. For the most part, our experiences in Illinois have been marked by such genuine acceptance, warmth, and love that issues of race have occupied little of our time on a personal level. We have been fortunate and blessed.

One can point to significantly improved race relations in many places; to fail to acknowledge them is to display a total ignorance of where we were in this nation fifty, twenty, or even ten years ago. The fact that my presence as bishop in Illinois has drawn little fanfare is evidence of how far we have come.

Yet there are reminders of the residue of prejudice, as well as a creeping resurgence of racism, and especially anti-black attitudes. Racism, like air, is everywhere in the American experience. One rarely escapes its omnipresent nature in all social structures and in every segment of the life of the church. This is no startling new discovery, but an acknowledgment of the depth of its sin, especially in America. Clearly, racism is not limited to the United States. No serious observer of world history can deny the global character of racism and bigotry.

What disturbs me most, however, is what appears to be a cessation of our national effort toward a genuine racially inclusive society. Even in my beloved

United Methodism, I detect a resurgence of racism. Few efforts are carried on anymore to bring congregations and individuals together across racial lines, and we have seemingly given up altogether our hope to foster interracial congregations. At the national church level, indications show a growing attitude to get on with the real business of the church, and the white liberal community seems to have forsaken totally the race agenda.

Others use the genuine need in the church for greater evangelism efforts and desire for church growth as a way to avoid their commitment to racial inclusiveness and the denominational commitment to confront racism. So they say the church must be about the business of evangelism and the renewal of spiritual vitality. No quarrel from me on that score! But I know what is really meant by many of these people.

The truth is that our denomination has had its greatest reverses in membership in no small measure because of the failure of congregations to evangelize in our major metropolitan areas, where racial and ethnic transition was and is occurring. If the commitment to evangelize were as strong as the commitment to racism, we would not have witnessed the almost wholesale closing of so many churches and the abandonment of communities.

The greater tragedy is that I see no evidence that congregations are doing anything different, although there is clamor about our need to evangelize. We dare not bask in a false security about the nature of race relations in our society or in the church as long as children still use words like "honky," "spic," "nigger," and "chink," and as long as adults and systems still relate to others as if they were less than fully human.

The words of the late President Lyndon B. Johnson are still appropriate: "We have come a long way. We have made a lot of verbal commitments. We have even changed a great many lives already for the better. But we are nowhere in sight of where we must be before we can rest."

I am forever haunted by those words from scripture, "And this commandment we have from [God], that he who loves God should love . . . brother [and sister] also" (I John 4:21).

A MESSAGE OF HOPE AND ACTION

On a scorchingly hot Sunday afternoon, the crowd seemed sparse, but the spirit was good. No sooner had we walked onto the statehouse grounds than, to my surprise, I was being greeted by United Methodists.

They were from Chicago, Springfield, and other communities throughout the state of Illinois.

The crowd at this peace rally—The Ribbon Celebration for Peace—was composed largely of women in the forty-five plus age range. There were more of us with gray in our hair than not.

Kim had come home the past fall excited that a local group had elected to join in the Ribbon Project.

"What is the Ribbon Project?" I asked.

I learned of Justine Merritt, a mild-mannered, but strong-willed, woman who had pondered the awesome potential of nuclear war. She knew she must do something, but what could one woman do? She embroidered a banner with the names of family and friends who would be destroyed in a nuclear holocaust.

Then she got an idea: What would it mean if banners for peace could be made all over the nation and strung together in one long ribbon? What if it were large enough to encircle the Pentagon? What a symbolic gesture for peace! What a dramatic and positive way to call for an end to a nuclear nightmare!

The idea caught fire. Soon banners would be sewn and embroidered all over the United States. In August of 1985, people would come by the thousands to stand with the Ribbon of Peace in Washington, D.C. Kim decided to add her banner to those from Illinois and planned for her trip to the August demonstration.

We walked the grounds and participated in the Illinois celebration at our magnificent statehouse. More than a thousand banners were spread on fences, wrapped around the stately pillars, and taped to the side of the building. Then, unbelievably, I saw one I recognized. It was Kim's, simple in design and message—a cross and bold letters that said "United Methodist Women for Peace."

In August, the length of the giant ribbon would stretch from Washington out to the Pentagon and encircle it, but more than that was accomplished.

People all over the nation prayed for peace. They studied about the horrifying effects of the nuclear holocaust. They engaged Congressional representatives in discussion, urging a halt to the manufacture and deployment of nuclear weapons—all because Justine Merritt could not tolerate the insanity of a nuclear war.

We can no longer tolerate a world that borders on the brink of total devastation. Each of us must do what we can, however small or insignificant we may think our individual effort. But we must act.

Labels like "hawk" and "dove" are irrelevant in the discussion about nuclear war. I hope that it is not even a partisan political issue, although I fear many will define it as such. For me, it is most of all a stewardship issue. God has entrusted to our care this beautiful, productive, and magnificent earth. We were given it to tend, to cultivate, to use, and to protect. It is not ours. We are to protect it, respect it, and love it; above all, we are not to destroy it.

A child who plays with matches long enough soon starts a fire, however unintentional. I fear we are playing with nuclear matches, and the risks increase daily that a fire of unimagined proportions will occur if the nations who possess these destructive forces do not soon find a way to control and cease the manufacture of nuclear weapons.

I want a world for my grandchildren and yours, a world of peace and justice. But if there is no world, no earth as we know it, peace and justice become meaningless. To destroy the earth or to watch it being destroyed without doing what we can to halt its destruction is to be a poor or an unfaithful steward.

On that hot, sunny Sunday in Springfield, we sang and prayed for peace. I stood between groups of Roman Catholic nuns, beside the president of a local United Methodist organization, a few feet from a group of mentally and physically disabled young adults and their counselors from Peoria. I saw children in strollers, men and women in wheelchairs, and others using walkers.

I saw the people of God. They represented people all across the nation and the world. I thought, "We dare not let this earth be destroyed—for their sake, for their children's sake and their children's sake, and for God's sake!"

We concluded the rally with a prayer that was used all across the nation on such occasions. It is a simple prayer but of significant import. I pray that you will make it yours as well.

> Oh God, lead us from despair to hope, lead us from hate to love, lead us from fear to trust, lead us from war to peace. Let peace fill our hearts, our world, our universe. Peace, peace, peace. Amen.

TODAY'S "LEPERS" ARE AIDS VICTIMS

The small, frustrated boy sat on a desk with an elaborate telephone system, straining to hear instructions from his teacher. The device, not yet perfected, did not transmit her words with clarity. He spoke to her and she to him. His eyes held no anger, just sadness. He has Acquired Immune Deficiency Syndrome (AIDS).

An elderly couple was being interviewed in their modest home outside Springfield. While in a nearby hospital for surgery, the husband had required a blood transfusion, and now he suffers from AIDS. All plans for retirement have now been forgotten. Lifelong friends no longer visit. The couple is lonely.

The fatal disease, once associated primarily with bisexual and homosexual men and drug addicts who use infected hypodermic needles, is now one of the most frightening and deadly diseases faced by the general population. Seen as an essentially sexually transmitted disease, it creates greater ambivalence. In one community, there was near hysteria as it was announced that an elementary school pupil with Acquired Immune Deficiency Syndrome has been permitted to attend school; the identity of the child and of the school have been kept confidential.

However this dreadful disease is contracted, its victims have become the new "lepers." They are isolated and rejected. Some are feared, and others are held in disdain. Those who know personally no one with the disease frequently view them as a category, a statistic, or a sinner. Many who want to be open, understanding, and even "Christian" need more medical evidence and assurance that the disease cannot be transmitted by casual contact. It is a complex, ambiguous, frightening, and heartbreaking situation.

I still see the little boy trying to get his school lessons in the isolation of his home. I read about young men who idle the day away in a lonely apartment, feared even by relatives, waiting for death, made the more difficult because they must wait alone. And I wonder: Do they have a church? A pastor? Are the children with the disease also denied admission to church school?

I understand now with greater appreciation the biblical lepers. Jesus "healed" or "cleansed" the lepers of his day. Indeed, he specifically instructed the disciples to heal lepers. How would Jesus translate that command today to us, his modern disciples, for these contemporary lepers?

An infant, a young boy, a homosexual, a retired husband—all these for whom Christ died need the loving compassion of the church. Each is a member of some family; each is someone's son or daughter. Each is precious, perhaps requiring love and acceptance from the Christian community more now than ever before.

As our scientific and medical communities search untiringly for a cure for this disease, I trust that the government, private citizens, and foundations will provide the necessary financial undergirding for costly research. I pray that we in the church will not be found lacking when those, our brothers and sisters, with Acquired Immune Deficiency Syndrome appear at our gates, seeking the ministry and love of the church.

We need no more lepers among us. There are already too many!

That little boy still hurts me; I'll never forget his face and the sadness in his eyes. Something deep within me knows it could be one of my daughters, or me, or even you.

SPEAKING THE LANGUAGE OF LOVE TO THE DEVELOPMENTALLY DISABLED

He always smiled and gave a rather subtle wave of the hand even while seated in the congregation. We were friends, although our contacts were limited to weekly worship services. Our conversations never seemed to go anywhere. I didn't know if he understood me; I rarely understood him. But we greeted each other with obvious and genuine affection. More often than not, we hugged each other instead of giving the customary handshake. He was a mentally retarded young adult.

I would watch him during morning worship services. He especially enjoyed the music and the choir and would sing with gusto. He enjoyed the church fellowship time following services, and he was excited by laughter and conversations, the movement of little children. He understood the language of love. Like all of us, he responded to it.

As I visit congregations, I see from time to time children and adults, married couples or families, whose mental development has been retarded. For physical or other reasons, known and unknown, the mental process stopped too soon, not developing with chronological age. When I see these precious ones, I know that they are, indeed, special. Many are functioning in ways heretofore thought impossible. Enlightened educational systems, more humane social services, and an increasingly sensitive society are making it possible for such persons to live productive and meaningful lives.

The church is a community of compassion that includes within it persons who might otherwise be ostracized or feared. Congregations must demonstrate this Christ dimension, this language of love that communicates in miraculous ways.

When one of our daughters was about sixteen years of age, she answered an ad in the newspaper, without our knowledge or permission, to be a companion to two mentally retarded children. After she was hired, she told us what she had done. We had the usual parental concern, which soon gave way to parental pride.

Our daughter's job was to take the youngsters out to the park, to the shopping mall, on walks, or to special events, such as the circus. She also bathed them each evening and prepared them for bed.

I remember the first time she brought the children home for us to meet them. We had all the typical apprehensions, but were overwhelmed when we learned that not only were the children mentally retarded, but also they could not speak. We watched in utter amazement as our young, unpredictable daughter communicated by the use of an elementary form of sign language. The children clearly understood that she was communicating more importantly with the language of love.

They normally got very excited, at least momentarily, when she brought them home with her. We would sit them down so that they could gain control of themselves. The little girl, who was about eleven, liked to sit on my wife's lap to have Kim gently stroke her head or arm. When Kim stopped, the little girl would firmly pull her hand back and begin the stroking motions again. It was as though each stroke were saying to her, "I love you, I love you, I love you."

Our daughter continued to work with those who were mentally and physically handicapped in summer camps and after school. Before we moved to Illinois, she was given the care of two men who were mentally disabled. Our anxiety heightened, but we marveled at her skill, patience, and love. She was even the driver and chaperone on their dates.

There is so much mystery in life, so much we don't understand. Why are some infants born healthy and develop and live typically normal lives, yet others are not? Why do others, as a result of some sickness or accident, have their development, physical or mental, abruptly halted? Medical science explains how it happens, but not why. What I do understand, however, is the power of the language of love to communicate in ways that touch the soul and reach the human psyche as nothing else can. I pray that in our churches that language will always be present.

THE AUTUMN OF THE PEOPLE OF GOD

But once us feel loved by God, us do the best us can to please him with what us like. . . . [Folks] come to church to share God, not find God. . . .

The thing I believe. God is inside you and inside everybody else. You come into the world with God. But only them that search for it inside find it. And sometimes it just manifest itself even if you not looking, or don't know what you looking for. Trouble do it for most folks, I think. Sorrow, lord. . . .

—Alice Walker
The Color Purple

ONENESS IN GOD RENEWED
IN A HOLY PLACE

Incense, an aroma that now suggests the holy, filled the sanctuary. Our family sat in the Cathedral Church of St. Paul (Episcopal) for worship and to hear the visiting preacher, a bishop from Nigeria.

Traditional Gothic sanctuaries have a unique quality. The brilliant stained-glass windows, with their reds and blues, grow more beautiful with age; the high altar with candles is a reminder that this is no ordinary place. The aged stone interior is evidence of strength and endurance. This is truly a sanctuary—sacred and holy.

I listened to this servant of Christ speaking with an accent from a faraway place. Yet, the words were familiar. He spoke of hope, discipleship, Christ, and unity. I knew deep within the true meaning of the catholic spirit. I was at home there.

God is made known in various ways, and Christ is worshiped in different settings. That God does not remain hidden and will not be boxed in defies even our categories. We attempt to make God Anglican or United Methodist, Baptist or Pentecostal. We attempt to make God American or Western. We debate whether God is three or one. We batter the deity about, declaring that God is white, black, brown, red, or yellow. In un-Christian ways, we badger one another, arguing that God is he, she, or it.

It all seemed so utterly fruitless as I sat in this holy place, assured that God is none of these and yet, mysteriously, is all of these. My mind cannot fully comprehend all that is God.

When he encountered God at Horeb, Moses wanted to give evidence to the people of Israel that he had indeed been with the Holy One. They would want to know a name, some description, some clue, but "God said to Moses, 'I am who I am. Say this to the people of Israel, I am has sent me to you' " (Exodus 3:14).

No culture can contain God. God belongs exclusively to no nation or race. God is truly catholic, truly universal. God belongs to no one, yet to everyone. Indeed, we claim God only because God first claimed us.

I should rather experience God than debate about God. The more I experience God, the less need I have for argument. Perhaps, if we spent more time in the presence of God, we would have less time to define God so precisely and so definitively.

A catholic spirit transcends all parochial inclinations. It reaches across nations and races, forms and rituals, languages and cultures. God is present and can be experienced in the awe and grandeur of the cathedral or in the profound simplicity of the meeting house, in the magnificence of a Bach chorale or in the power of a gospel chorus.

We are enriched by the diversity of expressions of worship and liturgies, and I am grateful that God's presence can be manifested in so many different and marvelous ways. I am at home wherever God's presence is affirmed and people worship and celebrate. Something transcends the form and points to the One in whose name the worship is directed.

Thus we are able to join hands with brothers and sisters everywhere in worship and praise to a good and gracious God, who is greater than all we can think and know and say.

CHURCH CAMP CAN CHANGE A LIFE

Sharon is excited. Talking non-stop, she jumps from one subject to another. Her conversations are becoming increasingly incoherent. She's going to camp in the morning. I had forgotten that eleven-year-olds still get excited about going to camp.

She has given me instructions on feeding her parakeets. I must say good morning, calling each of the birds by name—Pixie, Greenie, and Dipsie. She has packed and repacked; she has a new bright red sleeping bag.

I'm excited, too. Church camps and outdoor ministry are sometimes our best-kept secrets. They have served the church well. With so many activities competing for youngsters' time, many church camps face quite a challenge to remain viable and operable. But church camps have a special role and function and must be undergirded and supported by our gifts, volunteer service, and campers.

To have an extended period in a camp setting surrounded by the beauty and mystery of nature is an experience that all should have. I grew up in a large city. Nature was something to be conquered, not explored and enjoyed. We had an understood rule: If it crawls, kill it!

How welcome is a setting in which one learns of God's creation in nature. Camping brings early and lasting lessons of the cycle of life. One learns the value and function of each insect and that even "pests" have a role and contribution to the life cycle.

Sharon, I hope, will increase her perspective of the diversity of God's family. She will meet youngsters from varied backgrounds, local churches, and communities. She will not only discover the diversity of the church, but she will learn of its commonality and mutuality also. I hope she will discover how much alike we are.

So important are Christian camp counselors and workers—those who will apply the gospel to outdoor experiences; those who are committed to spending twenty-four hours of each day with excited, sometimes frightened and anxious youngsters; those who in the middle of the night will have to reassure a homesick youngster that all is well and, in so doing, will teach something about the caring community.

The evening, around camp fires, will be a time of reflection and a time to settle down after a busy day. Songs will be learned that will never be forgotten and when heard will always have a special place and memory.

Often, in these camp settings, the voice of God is heard in a special way. Some make life changing decisions, others get perspective, still others actually "find" God. Some have found their life mate at church camp. And while none will admit it, some held hands for the first time or received their first kiss at camp.

I hope that no youngster would go through youth without a camp experience. Parents, pastors, and congregations who recall the value of being at church camp should ensure that all young people have an opportunity for their own experience.

Church camps have broadened their programs and activities for a wider constituency. There are camps for those with special needs, language camps, computer camps, camps for families, and camps for single young adults. When a special need is identified, staff and leaders will explore the possibility of organizing a camp around that need.

What a privilege it is to be with others in the out-of-doors, exploring God's wondrous works—to gaze at the stars, to "hear" the quiet and silence of night and to relate it to a good and loving God, to make new friends and to grow, and to feel God's presence in this special way.

Sharon has every right to be excited about going to camp, and so does her dad.

THE SPIRITUAL AND SOCIAL MINISTRIES OF THE CHURCH GO HAND IN HAND

To be spiritual does not mean to be socially irrelevant. I note with particular interest comments that suggest that a pastor or a church ought to be "spiritual." On the face of that statement, I agree, but I profoundly disagree with its implication.

For some persons, to be spiritual means refraining from involvement in the affairs of the "world." "Don't relate to or speak to social, political, and economic issues," they say. "Leave these concerns to those who are experts in such matters. The church should stick to religion."

Why must one make a choice? In my judgment, one can be both spiritual and socially relevant. I shall go one step further and say one ought to be!

This sacred-secular tension has been with the church a long time. I obviously don't adhere to such a dichotomy. To divorce oneself from the hurts and realities of the human predicament is impossible if not irresponsible. How can a faithful church or a conscientious pastor ignore the surroundings? Can a church be silent about the farm and rural crisis? Or the threat of nuclear annihilation? Or a multitude of issues that affect the lives of people—mind, body, and spirit?

The church, however, is not a political or social agency. Its *raison d'etre* is to proclaim Christ in all his fullness. All the church is and does and says must reflect and point toward the One for whom we exist: Jesus the Christ!

Imagine Jesus as a resident of Peoria, Farmersville, Johannesburg, or New York. Can you see him reading the morning paper, watching the six o'clock news, and then ignoring all he read, heard, and saw?

Do you believe Jesus would be oblivious to the plight of factory workers, managers, and corporate executives? Do you believe Jesus would not speak to or on behalf of the forgotten and neglected? As he watched farm families disintegrate, do you believe he would stand by and do nothing—but be spiritual?

There would be no Methodism today if one named John Wesley had not become impatient with the lack of compassion and social relevancy of the Church of England of the eighteenth century. He was equally concerned that the church lacked spiritual vitality, that it failed to help the masses see the redemptive and saving power of Jesus Christ. John Wesley was moved to present a holistic gospel, spiritual and social, that revolutionized the church and religion of his day.

The church of Jesus Christ must first, last, and always be grounded in Jesus Christ. He must be the center. Jesus, throughout the scriptures, reminded his followers that the evidence of their faithfulness to him was demonstrated by their relationship to others: "I will know that you are my disciples because you love one another." Jesus urged that if we were truly spiritual, we would feed the hungry, give the thirsty drink, welcome the stranger, clothe the naked, heal and visit the sick, liberate the oppressed, and love those who hate us. He said that by our fruits we give evidence of our faithfulness.

A church that is not relevant in social contexts will lose its way. A church that is not spiritual has already lost its way.

CHURCH SCHOOL IS A FAITH JOURNEY FOR ADULTS

The church school class was interesting, the teacher well prepared. He had rapport with the class, and his easy style maximized our discussion time. From my observation, all members felt comfortable in sharing ideas. The lesson topic I must admit, "The Second Coming," was not one of my favorite subjects.

I am an avid supporter of church school, especially for adults. Attendance for children is expected, but for many adults, church school attendance is something akin to acts of supererogation.

I try hard to be in church school every Sunday. This particular Sunday was my first time to attend this class. Some reacted to the bishop's being in class; I tried to put them at ease. I didn't want my presence to be intimidating. Certainly, I did not want the group to assume that they had some biblical authority or theologian in residence. I said to the class that a bishop journeys in the faith as do all other Christians. Any response I made during our discussion was no more valid because I am a bishop. It was a good class; the time passed too quickly.

The teaching ministry has always been an important aspect of the mission of the church. I have enjoyed being both student and teacher at various times in my life. For two years, I taught the new members class in our church every Sunday except the first one of the month. I know I was more excited about these classes than many of the participants; I learned so much.

Church school is a rewarding experience. You are exposed to the thoughts and ideas of biblical scholars, noted theologians, and church leaders. With peers, you share your faith, your doubts, and your hopes. Church school, for me, has been an opportunity to learn from the theological insights of others. I am challenged to reexamine my own beliefs and, in the process, to change and grow. I have been forced to deal with an array of subjects that otherwise might not have gotten attention. Church school is an important nurturing experience for me.

I like the give and take of discussion. I welcome new ideas, and I am helped by those with a more mature faith than my own. Many times I have ventured into a church school class, only to find someone's eyes shining, telling his or her story about the Lord's work in a life or an event. Such testimony has lifted and inspired me.

On other occasions, I was so overwhelmed with personal needs and concerns that I overlooked issues and needs greater than my own. Again, a class participant or a lesson illustration helped me to see the faith more holistically.

I must confess that not every church school class is a winner. Some teachers and students are too dogmatic, too rigid, but I think they are the exception and not the rule. However, it takes all kinds of people and attitudes to make the world and church school class interesting.

In our faith journey, I am sure we can identify many sources of importance and strength. Among those I identify are committed, caring, and sensitive church school teachers and the church school, itself. These are rich resources of the church. Please don't overlook them or take them for granted.

BEING AT HOME WITH GOD'S PEOPLE

The opening prayer contained familiar words, such as *celebration, meaning, hope, God's presence, covenant,* and *peace.* I was immediately at home. I sat in the Shabbat service at one of the two synagogues in town. I was a guest, but for most of the service, I had a sense of belonging.

The ancient and contemporary Hebrew melodies sung by the unseen choir added a sense of mystery to the act of worship, as did the holy ark, in which the sacred Torah was kept. The doors were covered with a bright, multicolored design of an ancient tablet, upon which the Ten Commandments appeared in Hebrew. Behind the doors, all worshipers know, are found the most important aspects of Jewish worship and life: the Law and the Torah.

As worshipers moved through the service, so much was familiar to me. What stood out most, however, was the affirmation of the sovereign God and the recurring theme of justice.

The rabbi spoke and sang in English and Hebrew. Transitions were smooth, and those of us who spoke no Hebrew had the benefit of a prayer book in both languages. Yes, I felt at home here and was proud of the Judaic roots of the Christian faith.

The occasion that took me to the synagogue was the ceremony of consecration of the new rabbi. Tall, young, bespectacled, bearded—he looked every bit the teacher, the rabbi. Yet, he spoke as a prophet as well. I was reminded that we Christians are an Old Testament people as well as a New Testament people. Christ clearly said that he came not to destroy the Law but to fulfill it. There can be no New Testament faith without the Old.

It is a pity that so many rarely embrace their Old Testament faith and fail to affirm the Judaic basis of Christianity. It is sadder still that anti-Semitism is too frequently present in our Christian community.

I covet the need for more opportunities for Jewish and Christian communities to come together in friendship and mutual respect to affirm the common theme of our faith. Facing common problems together would be more effective in making the wholeness of life and justice a living reality.

As I sat in the beautiful, but simple, temple, I moved mentally from this to another temple long ago. I saw one who sat as a boy and later as a man in the synagogue. He would later teach, preach, and heal. The synagogue remained important to him. He found strength in it and in the scriptures. These he passed on to his disciples, and while many around him could not accept his claim or even his teaching, his message of love and forgiveness never changed. It remained to the end.

I looked around me in the synagogue and saw faces, none of which looked like me. I heard a language, spoken and sung, that was not my own. Yet, I knew in the most fundamental sense that these were my people because they were God's. None of us could exclude the other from God's family and God's love. It was good to be in this holy place, this temple of God's peace. I recognized anew the divine wisdom of God, and the closing words of the opening prayer spoke to this yearning of my soul:

> And may we become more than we have ever been, more than we are; reaching for a perfection beyond our grasp, growing and learning one day to make this day's peace for all days, learning one day to do justly, and love mercy, and to walk alongside the One who walks with us.

LABELS ARE A BARRIER TO COMMUNITY

Jesus said, "You shall know them by their fruits" (Matthew 7:20)—not their labels!

It is increasingly disconcerting how labels divide the church. In a denomination, unfortunately, labels become the manner by which the faith is authenticated, the worthiness of clergy and laity determined.

Liberal, conservative, charismatic, feminist, liberationist, holiness, social activist, evangelical—people take these labels on themselves or are given them. Sometimes they become signs of pride; at times people use them to denigrate or discount others.

I am neither impressed nor intimidated by labels. No label can encompass all that an individual is or aspires to be. Labels become a convenient way to avoid facts. If one knows your label, then, presumably, he or she doesn't need to learn any more about you. You have been neatly pigeonholed and categorized so that it is known what you think and believe on every subject and every issue. Nonsense!

Language and labels should help communication, not obscure it. Labels in our denominational dialogue can make communication and relationships more difficult. To be sure, we all have particular points of view, theological emphases, and social and political positions. However, these should not be the total measure of one's commitment and character.

What has happened to the quality of our Christian community? We treat one another as belonging to enemy camps rather than to a common fellowship with a common Lord.

I observe that few, if any, people or groups have all the truth all the time. In the broadness of the Christian community, all of us have some of the truth some of the time. Consequently, we need to listen with open hearts and open minds with the possibility to learn and to hear from others a truth we lack at a particular time or in a particular area. Therefore, if labels prevent the listening and learning process, they become destructive and demonic.

Labels also become badges of self-righteousness for the wearer. They are flaunted and brandished about as if to say, "I have it, and you don't." Some use it as a way of announcing their superior spirituality, knowledge, or theological wisdom. As I recall, Jesus had real difficulty with the self-righteous of his day.

Labels ought not to be given any more importance than they deserve. They are approximations, glimpses of what a person is or believes. We will not and cannot eliminate labels, but we can avoid the unfair manner in which they are used.

Indeed, our positions, while held with conviction, ought not to be signs we wear of undue piety. Neither should they be barriers to prevent dialogue and mutual respect.

I led a spiritual retreat recently, and as a part of our day together, I gave the group several exercises and assignments. One proved to be especially interesting.

I told the group to imagine that a decree had been handed down, declaring that all Bibles had to be destroyed. No one could own a Bible. However, each person could tear from the Bible one chapter only. Then I said, "Take time; reflect. Go through your Bible and select the chapter you would take." In small groups, members were to identify the chapter and share why they selected it.

I moved from group to group, listening to their discussions. I discovered that there was no relationship between theological labels and chapters chosen.

When people were forced to cut through an array of issues in order to get to the essentials of faith, they were not as far apart as they suspected. The labels worn or held were not as determinative as we might have predicted.

I seek to know you not by your labels but by your fruits. I try to see how Christ is manifested in your life—in relationships, speech, behavior, attitude, witness, and ministry. I seek the Christ I need to see in others. I pray that I will find him in you, whatever your label.

Finally we have but one label that applies to us all: Sinner.

LEARNING TO WITNESS IN A HUMBLING SPIRIT

It is disheartening to observe how much ill-will and actual violence are perpetrated in the name of religion. Rather than being the source of bringing the human family together, it has often served more to divide us. It is understandable why some find it difficult to embrace religion and the reality of a Supreme Being. In the name of God, there have been wars, executions, persecutions, discrimination, and segregation. Religious prejudice abounds even today.

Each religion, cult, and denomination claims that it has the final truth and is willing not only to die for it, but also in some instances to kill for it. Or, it is reasoned, unless one prays or genuflects, sings or proclaims in a prescribed way, then eternal punishment will be the just reward. Each group has its definition of saved and unsaved, found and lost.

Some parents disown their children who find another, more acceptable, way. Communities ostracize individuals who find God's truth in a different expression of the faith. Still others are condemned when they depart from the "faith of our fathers," all in the name of religion and on behalf of God.

I am prepared to let God have the final word; God will anyway! No denomination, no body of systematic theology will have the final word. Only God will have that final yes or no, and I trust God more than any religious order or ecclesiastical hierarchy.

That God's ultimate manifestation has come to me through Jesus Christ can never be changed or denied. I am compelled to share this good news because of the reality experienced in my life. This is no objective reality, but is a highly subjective one. Sometimes it is called belief, other times faith. But since it has made a difference, I dare not keep it to myself. The good news must be proclaimed. It must be shown as well as said.

The Christian faith is one that embraces rather than excludes. The Savior was always saying, "Come unto me." His arms were outstretched to welcome, not to turn away. Denominationalism ought to express the diversity of the gifts of the spirit and not the exclusivity of revealed truth.

Shortly after arriving in Springfield, I learned that the bishops of the Roman Catholic Church and the Episcopal Church had offices here. After meeting them, I proposed that we meet on a somewhat regular basis for morning prayers. I approached the question with some degree of apprehension, but reasoned "nothing ventured, nothing gained." I was elated when both bishops agreed.

Once a month at 6:30 A.M., bishops of three expressions of the faith meet for prayer. We pray for our pastors, congregations, nation, and world. We pray for one another. Around the breakfast table, we break bread together. Barriers fall; the fellowship is enhanced. It is a small step, but I believe God is pleased.

Jews and Christians have gathered in Springfield for a conference of significant dialogue with one another. I was overjoyed over Pope John Paul II's visit to Rome's central synagogue. The chief rabbi and the pope embraced and together participated in a special service, each reading from the book of Psalms. These are not insignificant expressions of the ecumenical and interfaith character of the religious community.

I was invited by my friend and brother in the faith, the Roman Catholic bishop of the Belleville Diocese, for a brief visit. When I arrived, I noticed at once that this was no ordinary visit. Something special was about to happen. The bishop and members of the diocese presented to me, the United Methodist bishop, a crozier (i.e., a pastoral staff such as what a shepherd would use) as a sign of my office and a symbol of our friendship and common ministry. What a gesture!

In a special edition of "Mission and Evangelism:

n Ecumenical Affirmation," prepared for the 1986 United Methodist Women's Assembly, is the following statement:

> Christians owe the message of God's salvation in Jesus Christ to every person and to every people. Christians make their witness in a context of neighbors who live by other religious convictions and ideological persuasions. True witness follows Jesus Christ in respecting and affirming the uniqueness and freedom of others. . . . We hope as Christians to be learning to witness to our neighbors in a humble, repentant, and joyful spirit.

I do sometimes wonder about heaven, and I have a suspicion that there will be a number of surprises when it is discovered who's there—and who isn't!

PEOPLE ARE GOD'S GIFT

God works through people!

So many times I have waited for a word or a "sign" from the Lord, expecting and almost demanding some dramatic sign. *Show me, God! Tell me, God!* Then God spoke to me through the community—the precious people.

One such person is Captolia Dent Newbern. It is she whose "principles" I quoted during my installation service as bishop in 1984. They are my working philosophy of life. Let me tell you about the person so that the principles will have greater meaning.

Everyone calls her Dr. Newbern. She possesses

more talents and skills than almost anyone I have ever known. She is one of those rare multi-talented persons who is as comfortable at a piano as at a typewriter. She is at home with national personalities or strangers on street corners in Harlem.

When I first met Dr. Newbern, I was a teenager growing up in Harlem, where she worked. She could have selected a far more comfortable setting for her ministry. She had earned four degrees—Bachelor of Science, Bachelor of Music, Master of Social Work, and Doctor of Education.

She was an inspirer. Somehow, she enabled one to dream great dreams, to set high standards and goals. She had a special rapport with youth and set high academic standards. She was always asking us, "What do you want to be? Where do you want to attend college?" Some never dreamed of going to college, but she expected it of them.

Captolia Dent Newbern always talked about the Lord. She unashamedly gave a witness to the Lord's presence and activity, and she forced us to talk and think theologically. Teenagers always crowded her office. What a magnetic presence!

Dr. Newbern was the first to say to me, "You're going to be a preacher."

The assertion shocked me because I did not fit any image I had of ministers. Besides, I wanted to be a lawyer.

"No," she said, "the Lord has something else for you."

She helped me hear God's call and then shepherded

me in a caring, careful way. She called me her son. God does work through people.

Her beginnings were humble in rural Georgia, where she was born granddaughter of slaves. Her parents were loving but firm; the family of ten children was close. Education and the church were "musts."

She expected us, too, to rise above our circumstances. I can remember her saying to us, "Make your stumbling blocks your stepping stones." Doubtless, this came out of her own early background.

Dr. Newbern went on making stepping stones out of her stumbling blocks, achieving recognition and honors, holding important positions in government, church, and academia. She was always an enabler, helping others to dream and to achieve.

She was a gift to us in Harlem; she literally saved lives. She imaged for me a faith of head and heart. She pointed me in another direction, personally financing a great portion of my college education. She corrected me and loved me.

In 1958, she left New York City; our paths did not cross frequently after that. I was just one of the many lives she had touched along her life's journey. But I never forgot Dr. Newbern.

By a set of unbelievable circumstances, I saw her in Dayton, Ohio, during the last session of the 1980 North Central Jurisdictional Conference of the United Methodist Church. She had decided to return to school and was enrolled in United Theological Seminary, Dayton. She has since earned two additional degrees, a Master of Divinity and a Doctor of Ministry. She is now 85! In a recent letter, she shared that she was off to England to attend an ecumenical conference.

Captolia Dent Newbern, the author, musician, educator, minister, humanitarian, committed Christian—how blessed I am that she touched my life.

Somewhere in your faith journey, you, too, have a special variety of a Dr. Newbern. Pause now and give God thanks for such persons, for finally, most of us are what we are today because a person has made a difference in our lives.

The Newbern Principles

1. As God's children, always love God and always treat every person as God's child.

2. Take what you have and make what you want, and your skills and abilities will always make room for you.

3. Never allow anyone to drag you so low as to make you hate, for hate destroys finally the hater.

4. Burn the midnight oil to achieve your goals and always study to become an approved workman of God; achieve excellence.

5. Have respect for education and stop not short of the highest possible level you can attain; in your faith and work whatever is for you, you will get it.

6. Develop a smiling face and always be gracious to everyone, even though everyone is not always gracious to you; and by all means treat others as you want others to treat you.

7. Stay with the church and be a person to work for change to improve the surroundings wherever you find yourself.

8. Your body is a temple of God; do nothing to mar or destroy it.

9. In all you do, do it to help somebody.

10. Always raise your eyes to the hills from where your help comes. God who made the hills, mountains, earth and heaven and everything in them can and will open doors for you that no one can open and no one can close.

THE CHALLENGE OF PREACHING IS AN AWE-FILLED RESPONSIBILITY

I marvel at the ability and resource of pastors who must preach to congregations Sunday after Sunday. Some make the difficult task look easy.

Most studies gauging the importance of pastoral functions reveal that the vast majority of laypersons place preaching and worship at the head of the list; yet, I think it is the most demanding of all pastoral functions.

To this day, preaching frightens me. I agonize whenever I must step into the pulpit. I always have a sense of not being totally prepared—desiring more time to fine tune a paragraph, to do more background research on a major point, to find a better illustration, to spend more time with God in silence. But eventually the preacher has no more time. The appointed hour arrives, and the congregation waits to hear the word from the Lord. How awesome!

The congregation is never homogeneous in needs or moods on a given Sunday. They come from everywhere, emotionally and spiritually. Some struggle with overwhelming grief and pain. Others have lost touch with the presence of God and look for a way back. Family and marital difficulties are so pronounced that merely performing routine tasks requires effort.

Many wrestle with profound and ancient theological questions, such as the meaning of salvation. Can one be saved outside of a belief in Jesus Christ? How can a good God allow natural disaster? Others simply want to be reassured by hearing the old, old story—familiar beloved biblical passages or stories remembered from childhood or days gone by. They want no disturbing message and only desire to be comforted.

Some sit in pews utterly angry with God, and often with good cause. The hymns and prayers ring hollow, and they come without knowing why. They do not expect, but desperately want, something to happen.

All sorts of conditions present themselves at worship, and the pastor is expected miraculously to speak to all of them—an impossible task!

However, each week the pastor stands before the sheep and, as the shepherd, leads them, not really knowing where all want or need to go. Sometimes both the pastor and the parishioners take this obligation for granted.

Often, congregations, bishops, district superintendents, and pastors become overly critical of the quality of preaching. We forget the nature of the challenge of preaching to the diversity of needs and the variety of spiritual experience in the average congregation.

Yet there are ministers who grasp the significance of that high holy hour. They labor and labor over the text; like an artist, they carefully stroke each line, sensitive to the needs of the people and to the shades and tones of words. In the quiet of the study, they talk it over with God, and then they break the bread of life. The expectations of the preacher are great, and the opportunity to do good is incalculable. What a responsibility! What a gift!

Those of us who preach must do it with greater care and grace, and those who hear with greater understanding and appreciation. It is an awesome task.

EXPRESSING GRATITUDE IS AN ACT OF FAITH

Giving thanks appears to be an easy act of gratitude. It ought to be, and for the most part is, for many of us. I have such profound gratitude to God that my songs of thanksgiving are unending; they overflow like the mighty Niagara. However, there has always accompanied my thanksgiving prayers a twinge of guilt and ambiguity.

The meaning of grace is essential to my theology and understanding of the work of Christ. There is no doubt that if the measure of my goodness became the criterion upon which blessings were bestowed, I would be a pauper, indeed. I can only explain an abundance of blessings as the grace of the loving Lord, who blesses beyond my worthiness or goodness. Herein lie the dilemma, the ambiguity, and the sense of guilt.

Of all special days, Thanksgiving holds a certain place in my life. I recall with fondness the rituals of Thanksgiving from my childhood: worship, shivering in mid-Manhattan while watching the famous Macy's parade, football, and family dinner. These are good memories.

The day was always permeated with prayers and acts of thanksgiving. I cannot sing "We Gather Together" or "Come, Ye Thankful People, Come" without wanting to shout praises of thanks and to recall those long-ago days and celebrations of recent years. Nevertheless I have been unable to escape the haunting sense of guilt and ambiguity about prayers of thanksgiving.

Thanksgiving Day will find our household filled with the aromas of the feast. There will be turkey and dressing, rice, collard greens, candied yams topped with marshmallows, baked macaroni and cheese, gelatin salad, hot rolls, and mincemeat, apple, and sweet potato pies. We shall gather around the table and enjoy the bounty of a good and generous God. As we give thanks, it will be difficult to hold back tears of gratitude.

Yet, I will be mindful as I partake of my plenty of those near and far who have little and of some who have nothing. If it is by God's grace that I am blessed with such fullness, why are so many left so empty? Why are they not also recipients of God's grace? I will wonder, even in my prayers of thanksgiving.

Good health, family, freedom, a nation at peace, colleagues—all are gifts for which prayers of thanksgiving will be recited. Still, I will remember the lands in which no peace abides, the communities in which farm family life is in shambles, those for whom each day is one of constant pain as body and mind deteriorate from some incurable disease, the young and the old who are alone with no family or friends and who are without the sounds of laughter and the warmth of companionship.

For the church and for my faith, these twin cornerstones of life, prayers of thanksgiving will be given. I will be mindful of places in which embracing one's church and proclaiming a faith are done at considerable cost. I will wonder why it has been made so easy for me. I could have landed elsewhere in life.

I trust that God will understand my gratitude and my guilt. It is precisely because of such overwhelming gratitude for the abundant life, not merely possessions but a meaning beyond "things," that my soul aches for those who know it not.

In this Thanksgiving season, as in those of the past, my prayers to a good and wise God and a loving Savior will flow, even though I do not fully understand this deep mystery of life: why some have so much for which to be thankful, and others have so little.

THE WINTER OF HOPE
AND RESURRECTION

Real, deep love is, as you know, very unobtrusive, seemingly easy and obvious, and so present that we take it for granted. Therefore, it is often only in retrospect—or better, in memory—that we fully realize its power and depth. Yes, indeed, love often makes itself visible in pain.

. . . Reality can be faced and entered with an open mind . . . and . . . consolation and comfort are to be found where our wounds hurt most.

—Henri J. M. Nouwen
A Letter of Consolation

THE JOURNEY TO BETHLEHEM TAKES TIME AND PREPARATION

Some years ago, it was necessary for me to spend most of December in New Zealand and Australia. I returned to the United States on December 23, exhausted after a vigorous month of travel, study, and exploration. The change from summer in Australia to winter in America was abrupt. My whole system was in shock, but I was not prepared for the shock that was to follow.

In less than forty-eight hours, it was Christmas morning, and I was not prepared! I had the strange, inexplicable sensation that I had gone to sleep on Thanksgiving and awakened on Christmas. I never got into the Christmas spirit that year.

Can you imagine not having a season of Advent, no time to prepare for the blessed Christmas event? Somehow, in my travels and activity, the time of preparation and the surrounding events that make for Christmas passed me by. I thus learned how important is that preparation for the Christmas event.

The Bible lectionary lessons, daily and weekly, telling the story of the coming of the Messiah, are important as preparation for his coming. To hear again the prophet's proclamation, to listen with the heart to the angels' singing, to stand in wonder with the shepherds and in adoration with the wise men are parts of the important journey to Bethlehem. The retelling of the story of God's most audacious act—to come in human form—is cause for the singing of hallelujah! The biblical events move from sacred history to living drama.

Advent and Christmas are not complete without Handel's "Messiah," I discovered anew as I sat recently in a beautiful sanctuary and listened to this most moving composition of George Frederick Handel. The words of Isaiah came alive as voices sang the ancient words and transported me to another time and place.

I know in the depths of my being that "every valley shall be exalted" and "unto us a child is born." The angels shall, indeed, sing, "Glory to God in the highest," and because we cannot contain our joy, the whole congregation will stand and sing "Hallelujah!" This is Advent! How much poorer we would be without it.

I know how important are the little human touches that prepare us and that I missed the year of my travels. There's the frustration and joy of choosing a Christmas tree and the disappointment that it doesn't look nearly as nice in the living room as it did on the lot when it was purchased; it had looked so much straighter, and I didn't notice that bare spot. And no one seems to like it.

As a family, we decorate, but first I must set the mood; I need Christmas music. So familiar carols are played and sung. We listen also to those contemporary songs that now have a permanent place, "I'm Dreaming of a White Christmas," "The Christmas Song," and many more.

Now decorated, with lights in place and traditional hangings, the tree really is beautiful after all. I missed that part of Christmas. I missed the shopping for gifts, wrapping and hiding packages. I missed the crowds and sounds of this holy season. I missed the all too temporary spirit of goodwill that seems to visit during this special time—the extra smiles, the special efforts to help one another and to express kindness in the spirit of sharing.

The season of preparation for the coming of the Christ Child is important. When one prepares spiritually and emotionally for the event, the culmination of it is filled with joy and fulfillment. I missed Advent one year, and I shall never take it for granted again.

NOTHING OBSCURES THE GOODNESS OF GOD

I am exhausted this morning after a busy week, but only the body is tired. The mind is alert, jumping from one subject in detail to another. The spirit is calm and there is a reassuring sense that the body, too, will soon relax and be at ease.

I look forward with great anticipation to this day. I am anxiously awaiting the sunrise; I have a magnificent view through our kitchen window. The sun rises over a huge soybean field; it is a beautiful sight to behold. How democratic is our God, for God gives every region its own peculiar beauty, and I have come to know the beauty of central and southern Illinois. I have discovered with great appreciation the beauty of the sky. The flat lands accentuate the sky, and we have breathtaking sunrises and sunsets.

My mother is a woman of great faith. I have watched her in the midst of tragedy and misfortune, disappointment and heartbreak, and she never ceases to amaze me with her unwavering faith. She has a favorite saying that in my youth would often annoy me: "God is good!"

During the quadrennial General Conference of The United Methodist Church held in Baltimore, Maryland, in 1984, I received an emergency call. There had been a fire in the apartment building where my mother has lived for forty-four years. I left the deliberations of the conference and made an anxious trip to New York City. When I arrived, I saw the signs of fire all around. Furniture and other burned belongings were on the street, water was everywhere, and the unmistakable odor of smoke filled not only the hallways but the street as well.

I slushed through water that had not yet been cleared away. With great fear, I walked into my mother's apartment. The door was open; the floor was drenched. Ceilings had caved in on this grand old building. My mother had covered her hundreds of little china "knick-knacks." Plastic was draped over furniture; buckets and pans were spread throughout in a futile effort to catch the water that continued to come through what used to be ceilings. The stench of smoke was overwhelming.

My mother greeted me with surprise, for she had instructed members of the family not to call. She reasoned that the General Conference was too important for me to be disturbed. She gave me a warm and strong embrace. I wanted to cry. Then she said, "You know, God is good!"

In the midst of such a deplorable sight, not knowing if she would be able to remain in this place that held for her so many lasting memories, she claimed the goodness of God. Absurd? Foolhardy? Naive? Hardly!

God is good! Even when circumstances are bad, systems unjust, people cruel, events harsh—God is good. It is a remarkable affirmation, peculiar and illogical to many, questioned by others, sometimes hard to believe by those who say they believe.

This morning, I have such an overpowering sense of the goodness of God. It breaks in on me and you when we least expect it.

Many are experiencing pain, grief, and heartbreak, and the tragedies of society and the world seem to multiply with each newscast. Never let these obscure your sense of the goodness of God.

Now the sky is a brilliant red as it cups an array of blue. My soybean field out the window—now I have claimed it—is a golden brown. Or is it orange? Our four parakeets are singing their familiar morning song, and my body is no longer tired. I am prepared to greet a new day and to meet God's precious people.

And I will be saying in my heart those familiar words—words that once annoyed me, but now sustain me—God is good.

A PLACE IN THE HEART
CALLED LONELINESS

I am lonely—not alone, just lonely. Have you ever had that sense of loneliness even when in a crowd or group? It sometimes comes upon you when you least expect it.

At times, a sense of loneliness can set in when you're in your own living room, even at worship or at a committee meeting.

Strangely, a sense of loneliness comes often when you are happiest, when most of life seems to be falling into place. At other times, it comes when you are feeling alone. But that is not the kind of loneliness I am experiencing now.

I am not talking about *being* alone, but rather about *loneliness,* that moment when you feel a disconnectedness with all about you. At times you feel you are standing outside of your environment looking in. It is as if the soul has temporarily left the body to observe all around it.

This loneliness is occasionally a sense of melancholy, sadness, perhaps even despair. For me it is more undefinable, so I try to understand its origin. Why, when life is so full, should I feel so lonely?

Is the subconscious prying itself upward to meet the conscious, reminding me how lonely leadership can often be? The weight of it is heavier than many realize, and in our most human moments, we forget how heavy.

Maybe the awesomeness of decisions made, and yet to be made, is connecting with that sense of inadequacy. Perhaps the pain of those spoken words or of that look hurt deeply and forced me to push the words and look into that region called, "It didn't bother me." And now, something in me is saying, "It *did* bother me."

Is my loneliness the result of a sense of frustration over South Africa? For the people being shot down in the street because they wanted to be treated as human beings? I have grieved so long for South Africa. As a high school student, I read Alan Paton's *Cry the Beloved Country,* and I have been crying for that country ever since. I fear for the future, for white and black alike; both are God's children.

Perhaps a sense of loneliness comes upon us because of the many demands and problems we carry, some of which we have not yet found answers to or resolved, and we ache with the hurt of them. We may not have been able to share them because some belong to others, and we dare not betray confidences. But they are heavy, and carrying them is sometimes lonely.

There are times when we cry without knowing why or withdraw and become quiet or moody. Some write great music or poetry in their moments of loneliness. Others find less constructive means to deal with this inescapable reality.

The Winter of Hope and Resurrection ||| *123*

This loneliness may be inevitable. Perhaps the Christian will always have these moments of not quite belonging. Is that why we are called a "pilgrim people"? Is this what Jesus meant by being in but not of the world?

I am growing to love Illinois as I have loved every place in which I have lived. You can never know how much "my" soybean field inspires me as I glance at it each day or how I feel a sense of pride when, from my window, I can see the capitol dome here in Springfield. I am becoming acquainted with the roads and highways, the signs and smells, and the places of this grand state. But this is not home. Neither was Washington, Maryland, Michigan, Massachusetts, nor even New York.

I think the soul has a way of reminding us that earth is not home no matter how much we love the surroundings and people. There is a dimension of the psyche or soul that knows this better than our cognitive or intellectual self. It tugs a bit because it longs for home, and it knows better than we that this is not it.

In the final analysis, loneliness may be produced by one or all of these realities, or perhaps none. Yet each of us, sometimes in our life journey, has moments of loneliness.

I didn't know it before, but now I do: Even bishops know loneliness. At least this one does, but it is a passing place.

Loneliness is neither a permanent place nor a devastating one, because I know that often in my moments of utter loneliness I have come closest to God. Nothing and no one else can fill that place at that time in the way the soul needs. God is able to reach me in those moments when I can rely on no one else, can lean on no other one but God, and I learn anew how able a God we serve, one who finds me even in my loneliness. Then I am thrust into God's care and grace in renewing and comforting ways. God speaks, and I listen because now there are no distractions. I am made aware of how dependent I am of God. Then, as strange as it may seem, I thank God for loneliness.

GRIEF AND HEALING IN A PARAKEET'S DEATH

Pearl died unexpectedly last night. As I looked at her, so still and delicate, I knew I was not prepared for the trauma it would cause my eleven-year-old daughter, Sharon. Pearl is one of four parakeets, who are her prized possessions.

Predictably, Sharon was devastated. Tears flowed freely, and as I held her close, words were inadequate. But I tried.

A child reacts to death as do many adults—disbelief, non-acceptance, questioning, anger, and guilt. We wanted to minimize the guilt, for Sharon's first question indicated that she felt responsibility. Of course, she was not responsible for the parakeet's death.

But she wondered. Had she taken proper care of her cherished companions? Should we have taken them to the veterinarian? She had constantly urged us to have the parakeets examined regularly. She took the death hard. She cried; I consoled.

Our routine morning schedule was now disrupted. We had to attend to more important tasks. We were dealing with life and death, love and loss, and with the "ongoingness" of life. These are lessons with which even an eleven-year-old must begin to grapple.

Sharon was still crying by the time the school bus arrived, so I drove her to school. We talked not so much about Pearl, but it was really all about Pearl. I just wanted to be with Sharon. I knew it would be a difficult day at school. She must function as if everything were fine in spite of the fact that two hours earlier, she had greeted the morning with the reality of death. Our good-bye kiss was special that morning. We both knew it.

In the afternoon, when I returned home, Sharon was preparing for Pearl's burial. She found a nice little box that only a few days before had held a beautiful corsage. She lined the box with tissue paper and gently laid the tiny parakeet inside.

Then Sharon did a remarkable and surprising thing: She wrote a letter about Pearl and placed it in the box. I have no idea what she wrote. This was between her and Pearl. It was her final word to the little creature she greeted daily, fed, petted, cared for, and loved. She was saying "good-bye" in her own private way. It was a profound gesture.

Finally, out the back door she went to find the appropriate place to bury Pearl. Somehow, she was not as sad now. She found a spot and placed the box in the freshly dug grave. She took flowers from a beautiful bouquet in our dining room and arranged them on the grave.

I left her alone. I could sense I was not needed. I did not know what would happen next. I tried to prepare myself, but I knew that with all my preparations I would still be unprepared. Then, with a sense of "everything's okay," Sharon hopped on her bike and rode down the street to play with her girl friend. She was learning about the "ongoingness" of life.

Somewhere in this drama of an eleven-year-old and a parakeet, mystery unfolds as well as certainty. It is not only a drama of a little girl and her feathered friend, but it is also a story about a father, a bishop, a church, and a world. It is about life.

In the drama, human emotions come together, sometimes colliding, other times embracing. We find answers as well as questions, contradictions, and hope. We meet the finite and the infinite.

In the drama's midst, I again see Christ. He breaks in unexpectedly, camouflaged, disguised. Once more I see him in an unlikely place.

AMID AWESOME PRESSURES, BEAR ONE ANOTHER'S BURDENS

I am saddened by the growing number of suicides. The phenomenon of teenage suicide is especially disturbing. The demographics of suicide are, themselves, perplexing. Those who no longer find meaning in life frequently have all the appearances we are led to believe make life meaningful—a good education, an above average income, the right neighborhood, a nice house, the best clubs, and all that many strive for as goals of acceptability and success. Young people have that added dimension of "their whole lives ahead of them." Whether in California, Illinois, or New Jersey, there seems to be a growing pattern to teenage actions, an effort to imitate their peers.

The reasons people find life not worth living are as varied as the people themselves. I offer no definitive analysis; more professionally trained persons than I are capable of providing it. I speak only out of an aching heart.

Some among us face awesome pressures of health, guilt, grief, and economic and vocational uncertainty. Some have lost perspective of reality or see reality altogether too clearly.

I wish I could touch these troubled brothers and sisters. However, they are closer to us than we realize—in our families, churches, communities, and schools. We often say, "If I only knew." In a real sense, we do touch them. We do know, yet somehow we miss the depth of their despair.

Our Lord said, "I have come that they might have life and have it more abundantly." I know the power of that abundant life. Consequently, anything that destroys or maims life grieves me, be it war, famine, violence, prejudice, or self-destruction.

Human beings are the crowning jewel of God's creative genius. Not only should we respect our own life, but that of others as well. We are to bear one another's burdens, not become a burden to one another by our insensitivity, self-righteous postures, or judgmental attitudes.

Rather, we should respect one another, try to understand differences, give one another more room to know and to grow. Parents must especially be ever vigilant not to place too much pressure on their children. That's difficult. We want them to excel, to accomplish what we, perhaps, were unable to attain. Yet, we must never lose sight of each child's individuality and capacity.

All of us live under too much pressure. We are constantly trying to please and accommodate so many groups, so many people. There are expectations galore, and we want to satisfy them all. What we need to do, however, is to slow down in this fast moving society and once again put life in its proper perspective. Position, prestige, power, and possessions have possessed us rather than the other way around. These may bring meaning to life, but they are not the meaning of life itself.

Those of us who claim the Lord of the abundant life must first let that claim be on our life and with Paul say with our very being that "in whatever state I find myself I will still praise the Lord."

To be sure, the pressures of life can become overwhelming. Problems seem unsolvable, redemption and reconciliation unattainable. Yet, at times the most salvific word is "Wait! Wait!" It is utterly unbelievable what time and God can do to the most hopeless situation. It is not just a pious promise; God can make a way out of no way. Momentary despair can, in a broader perspective of time and context, bring healing and hope.

We are not alone. Friends, colleagues, and family members can and will stand with us. I am certain, above all else, that the Lord is with us. He stands with us, not always to erase the problem, but to share its weight. He stands with us, not always to erase the darkness, but to give light in its midst. He stands with us not because we are good but because we are his.

That's the good news. Jesus came that we might have life and have it more abundantly. Share that good news with someone today. You may never know whose very life might depend upon it.

"PROGRESS" COMES TO THE SOYBEAN FIELD

At times, it is difficult to face reality. You know the inevitable, but pretend that it won't come or hope and pray that the outcome will be different.

I am losing my soybean field.

That open space alongside our house was a much-needed world for me. I watched the sun rise against the open field and found an unknown serenity. When sad or lonely or frustrated, I looked out the window on that field and gained a sense of hope and perspective. At other times, the sheer beauty of it lifted my soul to new heights.

But progress has come! My soybean field will soon be a new subdivision. Streets will be put in, houses will go up, construction crews will be everywhere. My neighbor's garden will be no more.

I knew all of this was coming. While the property was still in litigation, I knew that progress would prevail in the end. I am sad. I must now accept the inevitable, but it isn't easy. Change seldom is.

Only late in life did I discover the beauty of nature—rich soil, towering trees, beautiful lakes, and open spaces. I was more comfortable with cement than with grass. Skyscrapers were a source of assurance, and crowds were companions. Darkness was unwelcomed, in fact a stranger, and noise was quiet. Indeed, I was disturbed by quiet, not by noise.

Now I know the beauty of the fullness of creation. I will miss my soybean field; it taught me so much.

I suppose this is merely a new reminder of changes occurring across the landscape of America. Small farms turn into subdivisions, large ones into corporate farms. One way of life is passing, another emerging. There is both sadness and gladness, a natural cycle of life; it is called progress.

We are tempted to avoid the inevitable in life. I mean the inevitable—not the maybe—change, death, growing old, the new. Children will become adults. Some things in life are certain, although unpleasant to contemplate. Avoiding them makes reality no less real. One reflects, takes a deep breath, says a prayer, and then faces life with all its surprises, changes, and uncertainties.

For the Christian, facing change, however difficult, is not a solitary experience. It may be unpleasant, strange, fearful, and even painful, but it ought never to be lonely. Christ the comforter stands with us; his promise assures us, "Lo, I am with you always, even to the close of the age" (Matthew 28:20).

This morning, as I look over my soybean field, it is beautiful. The plowed, rich black earth does not know how much it has meant to this stranger who has adopted it. I shall have to take longer looks now, paint its picture on my mind and soul, so that when the day comes when there will be streets, houses, cars, and television antennas in its place, I will still be able to look out my window and see my soybean field.

I will thank God for letting me share it for just a little while.

IN LIFE AND DEATH, WE ARE THE LORD'S

Death sometimes comes too quickly. It does not allow us time to brace ourselves for its devastating impact. It arrives when we least expect it, at a time when the last thing on our calendar is death. We are busy living and enjoying the fullness of life. The awareness of our mortality is not uppermost in our consciousness.

At other times, death comes so slowly. One lingers in great pain and suffering, praying for relief; yet death takes its time. It does not arrive on schedule. The waiting is difficult for all. There is a sense of paradox, for it comes as the welcomed unwelcome guest.

Sometimes death comes too early. It snatches a

little one, a young adult, a promising student, a person at the height of his or her career when there's so much of life to be lived and enjoyed and anticipated. While, intellectually, we know that death will make its visit sooner or later, we don't expect it to come early.

For the most part, death is kind, even considerate; it comes to us in the appropriate cycle of life. It comes as the mind and body begin to feel the toll of life, when the parts begin to wear out, when dreams have been fulfilled and we have glimpsed a future not to be ours, when contributions have been made, love given. It becomes time to make room for another, who will experience the joy of life as we have experienced it. It is then that death comes on time.

Yesterday, death came too quickly. No one was prepared for it. Rather, no one *expected* it. My friend was full of life. We sat at the same table for lunch. We talked, joked, and laughed together and looked forward to our next visit. We did not in our wildest imaginings expect death to come so quickly. Not the next day!

Although death is as constant as night and day, it still seems an intrusion. We tolerate it but are not accustomed to it. When death does not touch us, we are apt to be more philosophical, more accepting of its reality. Perhaps its democratic character causes us the greatest stress; ultimately it touches all of us.

A part of life's definition is death; the question is when and how—not if. We prefer that it come on our schedule, but death has its own timetable.

The Christian life is one lived in the Lord. It prepares us for life, but it also prepares us for death. To be Christian does not make us oblivious to the pain of death, but rather helps us to understand its reality. There is the assurance that whether we live or die, we are the Lord's. This has a way not of decreasing the sting of death, but enabling us to endure it. Having endured it, there is the promise that we shall overcome it.

Although death comes too quickly sometimes, often when we least expect it, the Christian is always prepared for it. We are bewildered, confused, and devastated when it comes, because we don't expect it, not because we are unprepared for it.

The whole Christian journey is one of preparation for life as well as for death. I know this with all my being; I believe it with all my heart. But yesterday death came too quickly.

A FIELD MOUSE TRAPS A PREACHER IN HIS OWN WORDS

When my daughters telephone the office, it is my practice to take the call immediately. It must be important from their perspective.

One day, I was in a meeting with my top administrative colleagues, who constitute the bishop's cabinet, when my secretary called me to the phone. I hardly got my "Hello" in before my daughter blurted excitedly, "Dad, there's a mouse in the house!"

I did not think this too unusual; since my soybean field out our windows is now being replaced by a new subdivision, those little field mice will be looking for a new home. But why was she calling me? I asked in a half-stern tone, "What do you want me to do?"

Without hesitating, she responded, "Come home and get it!"

Since I couldn't go home, I assured her that she could handle the situation. When I finally did arrive, to my great surprise the girls had trapped the mouse under a wastepaper basket, but they didn't know what to do next. By now, Kim, my wife, had come home to join this fearless band of mouse trappers!

What now? With broom in one hand and carefully lifting the wastepaper basket with the other, I prepared to dispatch the little creature to "mouse heaven." I came down on it with a bang, then another. Our twelve-year-old, who had been observing this melodrama, began shouting through tears, "Don't do that! Why don't you practice what you preach?"

I was stunned. What else do you do with a mouse but kill it?

She dashed to her room and slammed the door. I stood with broom in hand, confused, curiously sensing a momentary guilt.

Why don't you practice what you preach? What a haunting reminder. What had she heard me say about life and death? Did she recall my words about violence and life taking? Clearly, her expectation was that my words and deeds should be consistent. That is a challenge.

Jesus reminded his hearers of this same demand: "Not everyone who calls to me 'Lord, Lord' will enter the Kingdom of Heaven, but only those who do the will of my heavenly Father" (Matthew 7:21 NEB).

Practicing what we preach is not always easy. Most parents teach their children openness, fair play, and acceptance of others as individuals. Then they choose friends from the "other" side of town, date a person of another faith or race, or take political positions that are clearly consistent with what was taught in church. They practiced what they heard preached.

Our faith requires not only that we say the "right" words, but also that we do the "right" deeds. Preaching, professing, doing, and acting go hand in hand.

Preaching and professing noble ideals and values are expected of Christians. Faith demands are often crystal clear, unmistakable. It becomes too easy in many circumstances to proclaim, "Thus saith the Lord!" Sermons flow, resolutions proliferate, pronouncements pour forth.

The constant struggle of faithfulness is to match our deeds with our words. I am continually reminded of this in my faith journey. There are always temptations to compromise, to modify, to ignore, to forget, or simply to fail. How frequently Jesus demanded performance as well as profession.

That little twelve-year-old of mine has a way of taking profound biblical and theological truths and in simple ways calling me to accountability. The nerve of her expecting that I practice what I preach!

MOMENTS OF WONDER AND ASSURANCE

Picture an anxious bishop atop a horse for the first time, and you have my portrait of a couple of weeks ago. I was talked into going horseback riding with some cabinet and staff members and their spouses. The real truth is that Kim said in her soft, charming manner, "You're going horseback riding!"

I thought it over and went horseback riding.

It was the most beautiful fall morning one could imagine; a touch of a "nip" in the air gave an invigorating urge. The sun was brilliant, the sky marvelously blue, the leaves golden and brown. Here and there one still spotted green leaves. It was a picture-perfect day.

I mounted my horse with an abundance of fear and uncertainty. In my mind, I had already played out the worst scenario: I saw the by-line in the church press, "Bishop falls from horse—breaks arm."

Some of the cabinet members had a special gleam in their eyes as they saw the fear in mine. But there was an unmistakable mood of joy as we prepared for our ride through some of the most picturesque woods I've ever seen. Yet I must confess that as we left the stables I was sensing that I had made a dreadful mistake. I'm more accustomed to riding subways and freeways than horses.

One colleague in front of me was an experienced

rider. He guided, coached, and assured me. Most of all, he was patient. Sometimes my horse would stop or want to go in another direction or munch on a few leaves. I felt out of control. The cabinet member would gently tell me to pull the rein to the right or to the left or just give a gentle nudge in the horse's side. He was a good teacher—decisive, clear, patient, reassuring.

At one point, he turned around with a smile. "One confidence you have is the horse knows these trails better than you do!"

How right he was! The trails through a heavily wooded area were breathtaking. Sometimes the terrain became hilly; in fact, we actually saw a canyon. What I recall most vividly was the symphony of the woods. Each animal, the river, even the leaves played their part in this music in its most natural form. I was now relaxed, not quite so nervous; I was enjoying myself.

Soon I was humming a tune, recalling words so appropriate for these moments. There was laughter, pleasant conversation, awe, and then my soul began to sing: "My God, how great thou art!"

We need to be reminded of God's greatness and goodness. We need moments of wonder and assurance. We are so often met with what appear to be insurmountable challenges; the "trail" seems so difficult, so unbelievably treacherous. Sometimes we sense that we are totally alone. Even when we look for God, it appears that God is absent.

The problems of the world on many days overwhelm me. The political complexities, economic uncertainties, and social disintegration appear insoluble. And there is often deep, personal private pain.

In the midst of this quandary, God speaks, acts, reminds, and assures us in many unexpected ways that we are not alone. Our ultimate confidence is that God does know these trails better than we do and does not, and will not, abandon us.

GOD'S FINAL WORD IS "YES!"

She was a cuddly little girl. She loved to give hugs and kisses. Her eyes were bright, her voice rather deep for a five-year-old, her smile the happiest you would ever see. She seemed never to get in trouble. Everyone loved Lorna.

Her parents are our dear friends and godparents of one of our daughters. Her dad was a staff colleague. We lived in the same community and rode together to work in a carpool.

One beautiful July day, returning home, having a fun time together after a busy day at the office, we were blocked from turning into my friend's street. No cars were permitted. I dropped my colleague off at the corner a block or so from home.

No sooner had I arrived home than the phone rang. On the other end was a terrible scream, "Lorna's dead, Lorna's dead!"

I began to tremble uncontrollably. Together, my wife, Kim, and I went to the home of our friends. Neighbors gathered. All I could do was embrace my colleague. Minutes earlier, when he had left me, he was laughing. Not yet fully internalizing what had happened, he tried now to comfort his other daughter and son.

An unattended car had rolled out of a parking lot, turned a corner, rolled down a hilly street, and caught two little sisters going to the mailbox. One was knocked out of the way, while Lorna was crushed to death against the mailbox.

As I drove my friend to a nearby university so that we could share this horrible news with his wife, I wondered about life, fate, and God. This inexplicable event tested faith; indeed, it caused some to question God. I did.

Two years ago, a United Methodist clergywoman was tragically murdered. Her ministry had been a remarkable one. She took a difficult, dying inner city congregation in Louisiana and turned it into a thriving, relevant ministry. Her congregation grew from 126 to 2,250 members, thereby making her the only woman in the denomination to serve a congregation of this size as its pastor.

Hers was a helping ministry. Those who faced a marginal existence knew they could always turn to her. She would be there with a hand, a prayer, a word of counsel, or food; she gave whatever seemed to be needed.

Her ministry is a model for other congregations and pastors—serving, selfless, Christ-centered, caring. It made no sense that such a faithful servant should meet such a tragic end. Why would anyone murder a sixty-seven-year-old woman?

William H. Willimon, in his book *Sighing for Eden: Sin, Evil, and the Christian Faith,* raises the ancient question: "The Judeo-Christian heritage affirms the goodness and omnipotence of God, and yet there is this evil in the world. How do we account for that?"

Frankly, I'm sure that having an explanation does not ease the pain. The loss is so great, so overwhelming, that to know why is still more descriptive than explanatory. There will always be a "why" after every explanation.

The tragic deaths of two of God's children, one at the beginning of life's cycle, the other nearing the end, are Good Friday events no matter what time of the year they occur. It is the world's final answer to life, or perhaps its final question.

But Easter is God's last word. When events, circumstances, and people have done all they can, when explanations have been carried to infinity, when hope turns to hopelessness, God reminds us that God is indeed the Alpha and the Omega. Death is not the final answer for the Christian, but life! When, on the third day, our Lord arose, God was rewriting history by the bold assertion that not even the best or the worst that life could give could compare with the mighty power of God.

We sing "Hallelujah" because we know that Easter means that God's final word is not an inexplicably tragic death but everlasting life. However the body ends its journey on this earth, or at whatever age the end comes for the Christian, it is really the beginning.

We celebrate the resurrection of our Lord and by it

affirm that God's final word is victory over unconquerable death.

Come Easter Sunday in the beautiful prairie spring, I shall sing and remember all those whose lives have touched mine, those whom I miss terribly—a little girl, a colleague, a family member. Through my tears, I will thank God for the Easter events, for God's final "yes" to life.